Ian Gillan

A Visual Biography

Andy Francis

Ian Gillan

A Visual Biography

Andy Francis

WP
WYMER
PUBLISHING
Bedford, England

First published in Great Britain in 2019
by Wymer Publishing
www.wymerpublishing.co.uk
Tel: 01234 326691
Wymer Publishing is a trading name of Wymer (UK) Ltd

Copyright © 2019 Wymer Publishing.
This edition 2023

ISBN: 978-1-915246-21-9

The Author hereby asserts his rights to be identified
as the author of this work in accordance with sections
77 to 78 of the Copyright, Designs & Patents Act 1988.

All rights reserved. No part of this publication may be
reproduced or transmitted in any form or by any means,
electronic or mechanical, including photocopying, or any
information storage and retrieval system, without written
permission from the publisher.

This publication is sold subject to the condition that it shall not,
by way of trade or otherwise, be lent, re-sold, hired out or
otherwise circulated without the publishers prior consent in any
form of binding or cover other than that in which it is published
and without a similar condition including this condition
being imposed on the subsequent purchaser.

Every effort has been made to trace the copyright holders of the
photographs in this book but some were unreachable. We would
be grateful if the photographers concerned would contact us.

Design by Andy Bishop/1016 Sarpsborg
Printed and bound by Halstan, Amersham, Buckinghamshire.

A catalogue record for this book is available from the British Library.

Contents

Episode Six: Here, There And Everywhere, 1962-69 — **9**

Episode Seven: Place In Line, 1969-73 — **23**

Episode Eight: Music In My Head, 1973-78 — **47**

Episode Nine: Secret Of The Dance, 1978-82 — **61**

Episode Ten: Zero The Hero, 1983-84 — **75**

Episode Eleven: Back In The Game, 1984-89 — **79**

Episode Twelve: Long And Lonely Ride, 1989-92 — **89**

Episode Thirteen: Ramshackle Man, 1992-1994 — **95**

Episode Fourteen: Sometimes I Feel Like Screaming, 1994-2002 — **101**

Episode Fifteen: All The Time In The World, 2002-2023 — **109**

Episode Six in 1966. From left: Ian, Graham Carter, Sheila Carter, Harvey Shield, Tony Lander and Roger Glover.

Episode Six:
Here, There And Everywhere, 1962-69

"I was a boy soprano in the Church Choir. Just one of those things… so music was very important and there was little in the way of media: you had to make your own entertainment. every house had a piano, every pub had a piano so everyone used to gather round and would sing folk songs and a bit later on also blues. I think I really started thinking about professionalism when I joined Episode Six in 1965. Up until then I realised the frustrations of not having the right equipment, not having the right transport, not having the right agent, not having all those things you dream of when you're a semi-professional but you don't understand what you're missing because you've never had it. I think it was in the summer of '65 when I felt like a professional for the first time."

18th October 2010. Interview with Menno von Brucken Fock for DPRP.net

It could be argued that Ian Gillan had a distinct advantage over many others. Growing up in the London area there was a hotbed of musical talent in the late fifties and early sixties. From those who congregated and performed at the 2I's Coffee Bar in Soho, such as Tommy Steele, Cliff Richard and Johnny Kidd, to the likes of The Who, The Kinks and The Rolling Stones, London was the centre of the British music scene that developed through inspiration from the blues and rock 'n' roll performers of America.

Future Deep Purple members Nick Simper and Ritchie Blackmore were also from the same West London area that Ian hailed from and it was probably inevitable that eventually Ian would wind up crossing paths with such musicians.

Like so many of the aforementioned musicians, Ian initially took his cue from America and in particular Elvis Presley, who first came to the attention of the UK public with his debut single release 'Heartbreak Hotel' in 1956. Ian was just ten but followed Presley's every move as closely as possible over the next few years.

By the age of 17 Ian had joined his first band Garth Rockett & The Moonshiners. Taking on a stage name was the done thing at the time; Brook Benton, Eden Kane, Duffy Power and Billy Fury were just a few of the many who didn't use their real names. Although The Moonshiners were only around for a month or so Ian tried his hand at a different name with his next band The Javelins. Originally calling himself Jess Thunder, then Jess Gillan, before eventually reverting to his birth name.

At least with the Javelins he was in a band that stuck together for a bit longer – from October '62 and through the Beatlemania period to March '64. His next move was to join Wainwright's Gentlemen which lasted for just under a year. Despite the name the band also included a joint female lead vocalist in the guise of Ann Cully.

Between November '64 to April '65 the band gigged extensively, predominantly around West London and the surrounding counties. They even recorded three numbers in March '65: 'Ain't That (Just Like Me)', 'Que Sera Sera' and 'Slow Down'.

After a gig on 26th April at the Seagull Hotel, Southall, Middlesex, according to archivist Nick Warburton, Ian Gillan quit to form his own group, Ian Gillan & The Dragsters. However, soon after performing a gig on 20th May, he joined the fully professional outfit Episode Six.

Episode Six had already been going since July '64 with lead singer Andy Ross, who Ian replaced. Soon after Ian had joined the band, Episode Six secured a recording contract with Pye Records. They would go on to cut ten singles up to early 1969 as well as numerous radio sessions and countless gigs. As Ian's quote here shows, it was the first band where he realised that music would be a fulfilling career. Although It's fair to say that at this stage, he still could not have imagined just how great his career would become.

"My grandad was an opera singer. He was a great baritone. It was quite amazing and the guy next door was a sea captain called Monty Lloyd and he was a tenor. They would do arias in the summer with the windows open while they were shaving in the morning you could hear them down the street. It was like living in an Italian village. It was unbelievable. I thought it was amazing. absolutely fantastic. My uncle was a jazz pianist too. He used to play boogie-woogie in stride and I was a boy soprano in the church choir, so pick the bones out of that."
Interview with Mark Dean, Antiheromagazine.com, 17th September 2016

The Javelins in 1964.
Left to Right: Gordon Fairminer (lead guitar), Keith Roach (drums), Ian, Tony Tacon (rhythm guitar) and Tony Whitfield (bass)

After quitting The Javelins Ian joined Wainwright's Gentlemen a seven-piece band consisting of fellow lead vocalist Ann Cully, Jim Searle (lead guitar), Alfred Fripp (rhythm guitar), Dave Brogden (tenor saxophone), Jan Frewer (bass, vocals) and Phil Kenton (drums).

By May '65 he had joined Episode Six, his first, seriously professional band with a manager and an agency. For the next four years Ian developed his talent with Episode Six as well as forging a close friendship and a writing partnership with bassist Roger Glover.

Fortunately, largely due to one fan, Wendy Ford, this part of Ian's career was visually documented. Wendy's photo collection came into the possession of Nigel Lees, director of Top Sounds Records Limited. Most are published here for the first time.

Another shot of The Javelins. Ian back left, Tony Tacon back right. In front of them from back to front: Gordon Fairminer, Keith Roach and Tony Whitfield.

From left: Harvey Shield, Roger Glover, Ian, Tony Lander, Graham Carter and Sheila Carter sitting.

Pictorial Press Ltd / Alamy Stock Photo

Twice in 1966 Episode Six performed at the Brand's Hatch racetrack in Kent as part of the Radio London Trophy meetings, sponsored by the pirate radio station, Radio London. The concerts were performed after the race meetings. At the first one in June, Episode Six shared the bill with John McCoy's Crawdaddies and David Bowie & The Buzz. It should be pointed out that Crawdaddies' vocalist John McCoy is not the same McCoy who joined Ian's band in 1978!

Brand's Hatch 19th June 1966

Brand's Hatch 25th September 1966

Biggin Hill Air Display, 13th May 1967

Wendy Ford / © Nigel Lees

Wendy Ford / © Nigel Lees

Brand's Hatch 18th June 1967

Savoy Rooms, Catford 28th October 1967

Wendy Ford / © Nigel Lees

Not everyone dressed like this in 1967 but The Moody Blues' Justin Hayward and Ian happily did so for a fashion shoot.

By mid 1967 there was a line-up change with new drummer John Kerrison.
From left: John Kerrison, Ian, Sheila Carter, Tony Lander, Graham Carter and Roger Glover.

Bromley County School, 2nd December 1967.

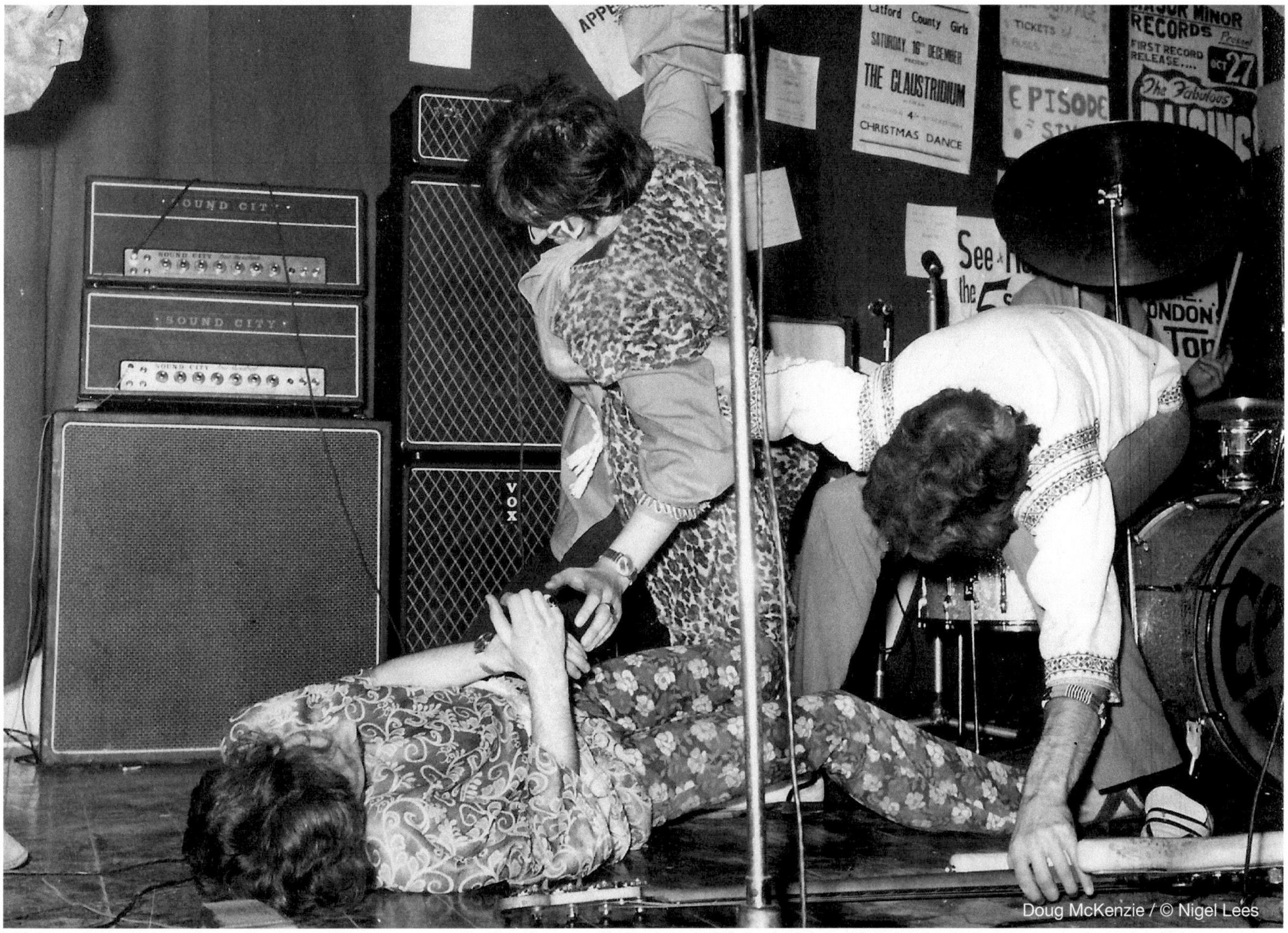

This photo captures Ian, Roger and Graham fighting. This was a bit of choreographed silliness they indulged in during Sheila's organ solo in their version of the Doors' 'Light My Fire'.

Luton Boys Club, 6th April 1968

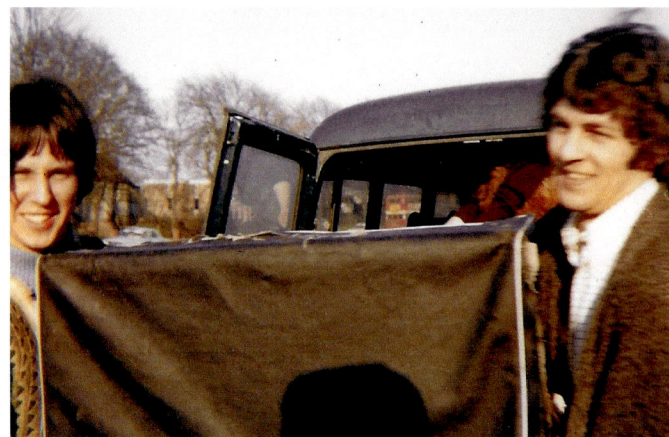

Wendy Ford / © Nigel Lees

Keys Hall Brentwood, 8th June 1968

Richmond Athletic Ground, 29th June 1968

Ian sometimes played the organ when Sheila took the lead vocal.

Wendy Ford / © Nigel Lees

Silver End Hotel, Braintree, 18th August 1968

By the summer of '68, the hair and whiskers were getting longer. Also the band had a new drummer in the shape of Mick Underwood, who more than a decade later would be back with Ian in Gillan.

Wendy Ford / © Nigel Lees

University College, London, 19th October 1968

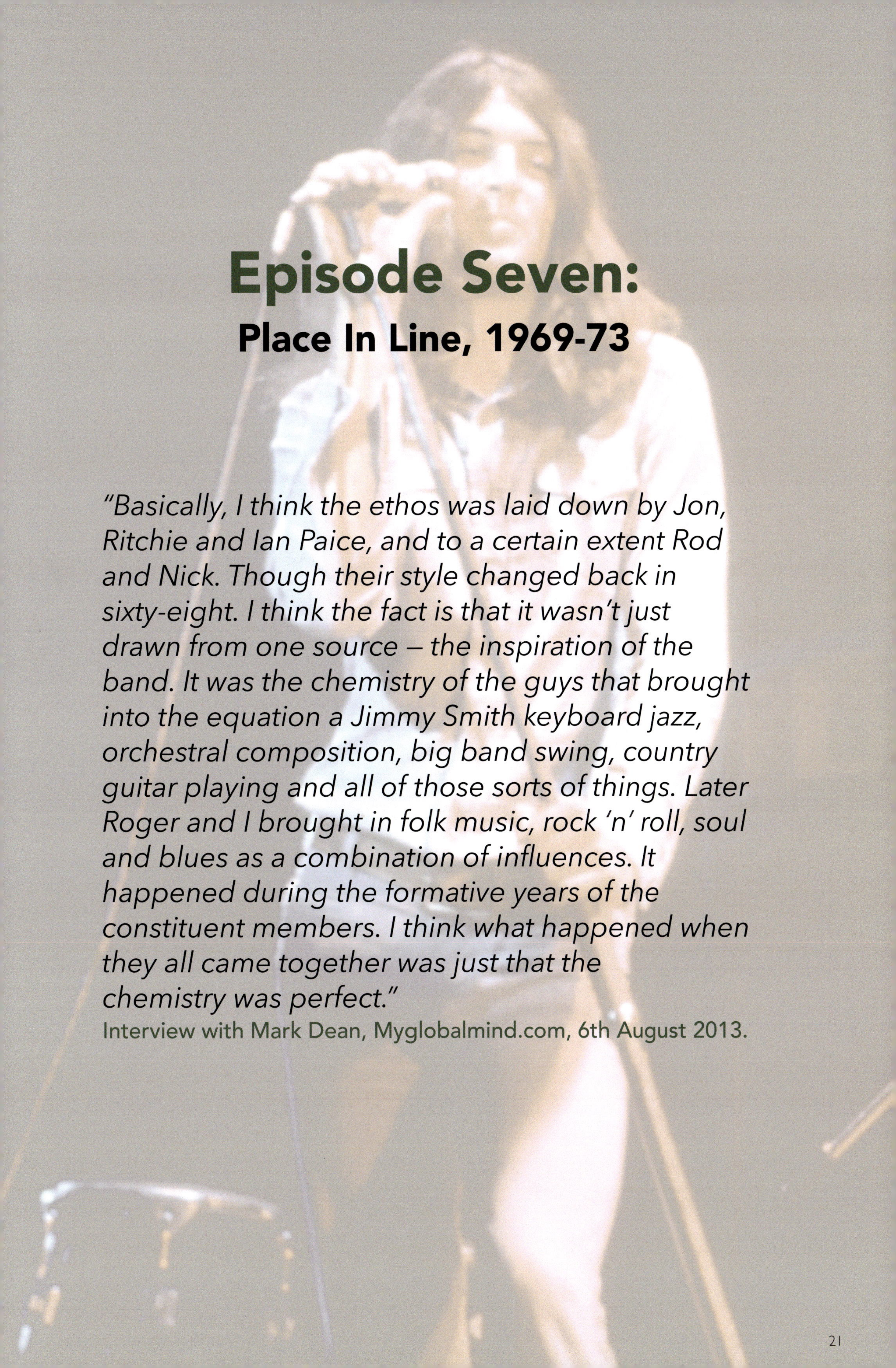

Episode Seven:
Place In Line, 1969-73

"Basically, I think the ethos was laid down by Jon, Ritchie and Ian Paice, and to a certain extent Rod and Nick. Though their style changed back in sixty-eight. I think the fact is that it wasn't just drawn from one source – the inspiration of the band. It was the chemistry of the guys that brought into the equation a Jimmy Smith keyboard jazz, orchestral composition, big band swing, country guitar playing and all of those sorts of things. Later Roger and I brought in folk music, rock 'n' roll, soul and blues as a combination of influences. It happened during the formative years of the constituent members. I think what happened when they all came together was just that the chemistry was perfect."
Interview with Mark Dean, Myglobalmind.com, 6th August 2013.

The coming together of Ian and his fellow Episode Six band member and writing partner Roger Glover with Ritchie Blackmore, Jon Lord and Ian Paice was a defining moment in Ian's and Deep Purple's career. Although they debuted at London's Speakeasy on 10th July 1969, Ian and Roger still had commitments to Episode Six and for a short while continued gigging with them as well as with Deep Purple.

But Ian and Roger also immediately set to work, contributing their writing skills to what would become the next Deep Purple album and the one that truly defined the band. A slight detour with Jon Lord's *Concerto For Group & Orchestra* in September '69 provided great publicity for the band but the release of *Deep Purple In Rock* in the summer of 1970 truly introduced Deep Purple in their homeland, where up to that point they had largely been ignored, as well as building a huge fan base across Europe.

Looking at it now, the four years of Ian's first stint with Deep Purple is a tiny part of his entire career but the body of work and the level of live performances was for many the defining period of Ian's career. Following In Rock, three more studio albums, *Fireball, Machine Head* and *Who Do We Think We Are*, along with the seminal double live album *Made In Japan* cemented Deep Purple as one of the era defining and most successful rock acts of all time.

Let's not forget that Ian also worked on one or two other projects during this time. Although his superb vocal performances on the rock opera *Jesus Christ Superstar* was recorded in one afternoon session, Deep Purple's management elected to negotiate a royalty deal rather than a session fee and it worked hugely in Ian's favour. The album topped the U.S. Billboard album chart in 1971 and has gone on to sell millions of copies worldwide.

In 1972 Ian also produced the one and only album by the British band Jerusalem that included bassist Paul Dean, the brother of his then girlfriend Zoë. The same year Ian also produced several songs for a potential animation project called Cherkazoo although it never reached fruition.

Sadly the sheer volume of work and the inevitability of spending so much time in the company of band mates fractured relationships and something had to give. Ian, having felt the band had gone as far as it could, decided to quit in 1972 but graciously agreed to see out commitments until an already planned Japanese tour in June 1973.

An early shot of Deep Purple at Southall Community Centre in 1969 where they rehearsed and where songs like 'Speed King' and 'Child In Time' were formulated. Those songs in particular quickly found their way into the live show once Ian had joined the band.

One of those early shows for Ian with Deep Purple was at the Bilzen Jazz Festival on 22nd August. As can be seen from the photos, the outdoor festival was not blessed with good weather. Indeed some of the acts encountered power cuts and delays in the show. It was also recorded by Belgium TV, the earliest known footage of Ian with Deep Purple. Interestingly of the other acts on earlier in the day was Marsha Hunt that included Nick Simper, so soon after having been ousted and replaced with Roger Glover who Ian had brought along to his first session.

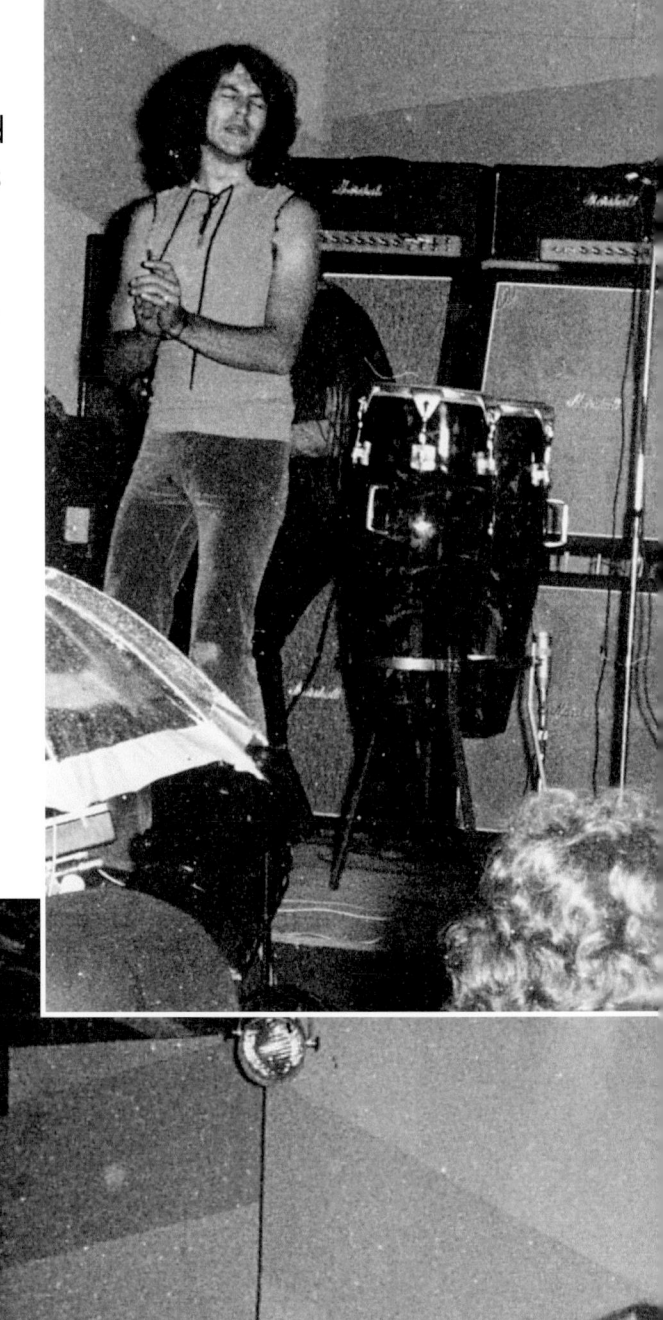

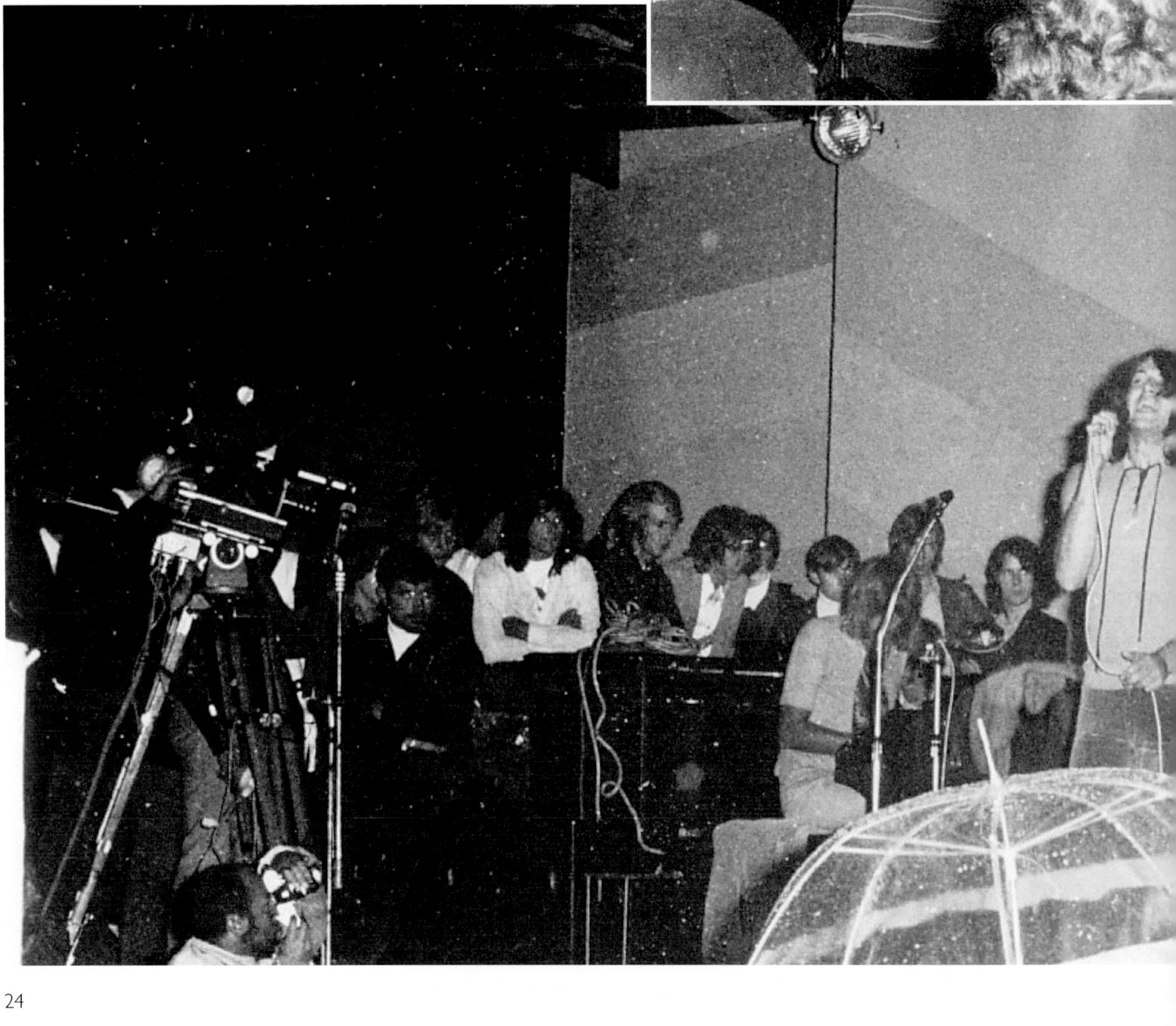

Paris, La Taverne de L'Olympia, 8th October 1970

© Philippe Gras / Le Pictorium (Alamy Stock Photo)

Ian has regularly made the point that Deep Purple is essentially an instrumental band. Whilst that undoubtedly plays down his own importance within the group, he was always happy to play the conga drums whenever Ritchie or Jon would play their lengthy solos such as at this show in Paris that was filmed by French TV.

Pictorial Press Ltd / Alamy Stock Photo

Ian snapped at De Lane Lea Studios in Holborn, London during the making of the promotional film for 'Black Night'.

Performing at the Gibus Club in Paris, 1st November 1970. This was the second gig that night. Deep Purple had played at the Olympia Theatre and after the show were invited to do another gig at the Gibus Club. Even though it is documented as the 1st, the gig certainly would have finished in the early hours of the 2nd, even if it started on the 1st.

Pictorial Press Ltd / Alamy Stock Photo

As Ian has often commented, he used to room with Ritchie in the early days.

Marka Press Holland (Alamy Stock Photo)

© Tony Burrett Photography (Courtesy of DPO)

From the photo session for the *Fireball* album. Although the band in general, did not think it was as strong as *In Rock*, Ian has always cited it as one of his favourites. Certainly from a lyrical point of view the album was far more adventurous.

Palasport, Rome, 25th May 1971

CAUGHT IN THE ACT

AFTER four months' absence from the concert halls, Deep Purple are back with a new act, new equipment and enough new songs to have made their latest album a double album.

Their three-week tour opened at Portsmouth's Guildhall on Monday and predictably it was a full house, surrounded by illegal poster-sellers and the odd ticket tout. And these boys only turn out when they know they're on to a sure thing.

Inside the hall the concert was delayed because supporting group Bullet's PA system hadn't turned up. Eventually taking the stage using Purple's amps, they proved a competent support act, heavy and loud with veteran bassist Johnny Gustafson leading them on.

But it was Purple the crowd wanted to hear and the cheers as they walked off stage must have been heard on the flagships in the harbour. They opened with the newest song in their repertoire — they wrote it on the coach travelling down — called "Highway Star," but the vocal balance was off-key and Ian Gillan's voice was barely audible.

With the controls reset they pounded through "Strange Kinda Woman," with an ear-splitting solo from Ritchie Blackmore. It was, in fact, to be Ritchie's night, for again and again he took the solos from Jon Lord and his arm pointing seemed to signify that he was in command of the group. He ended the set by flinging his two guitars around, which never fails to excite an audience.

"No, No, No," from their new album, promises to be a favourite live number, while "The Mule," another new track, has been transformed into a vehicle for Ian Paice's drum solo. "Child In Time" is the only number retained from their old act although for an encore they chose "Speed King" and a second encore was their wild version of Little Richard's "Lucille."

A brand new PA system, which the group bought last week, wasn't working properly on the night, so Purple used older equipment but when these sound problems are ironed out, Purple look like doing their best-ever business in this country — CHRIS CHARLESWORTH

DEEP PURPLE'S IAN GILLAN and RITCHIE BLACKMORE: new act

Purple patch

At the Rainbow Theatre where the front cover for *Made In Japan* was actually shot.

At the height of Purple's success in 1972. The year *Machine Head* was released and at the end of the year the phenomenal double live *Made In Japan* as well. Ian was unhappy with his vocal performance on the album, but for most people he had no reason to be.

A little percussion interlude with Roger during the last American tour.

Everett Collection Inc (Alamy Stock Photo)

During the final American tour at Long Beach Arena, California on 15th April 1973.

© Jeffrey Mayer Pictorial Press Ltd (Alamy Stock Photo)

In Japan for the final farewell.
Courtesy DPO

Courtesy DPO

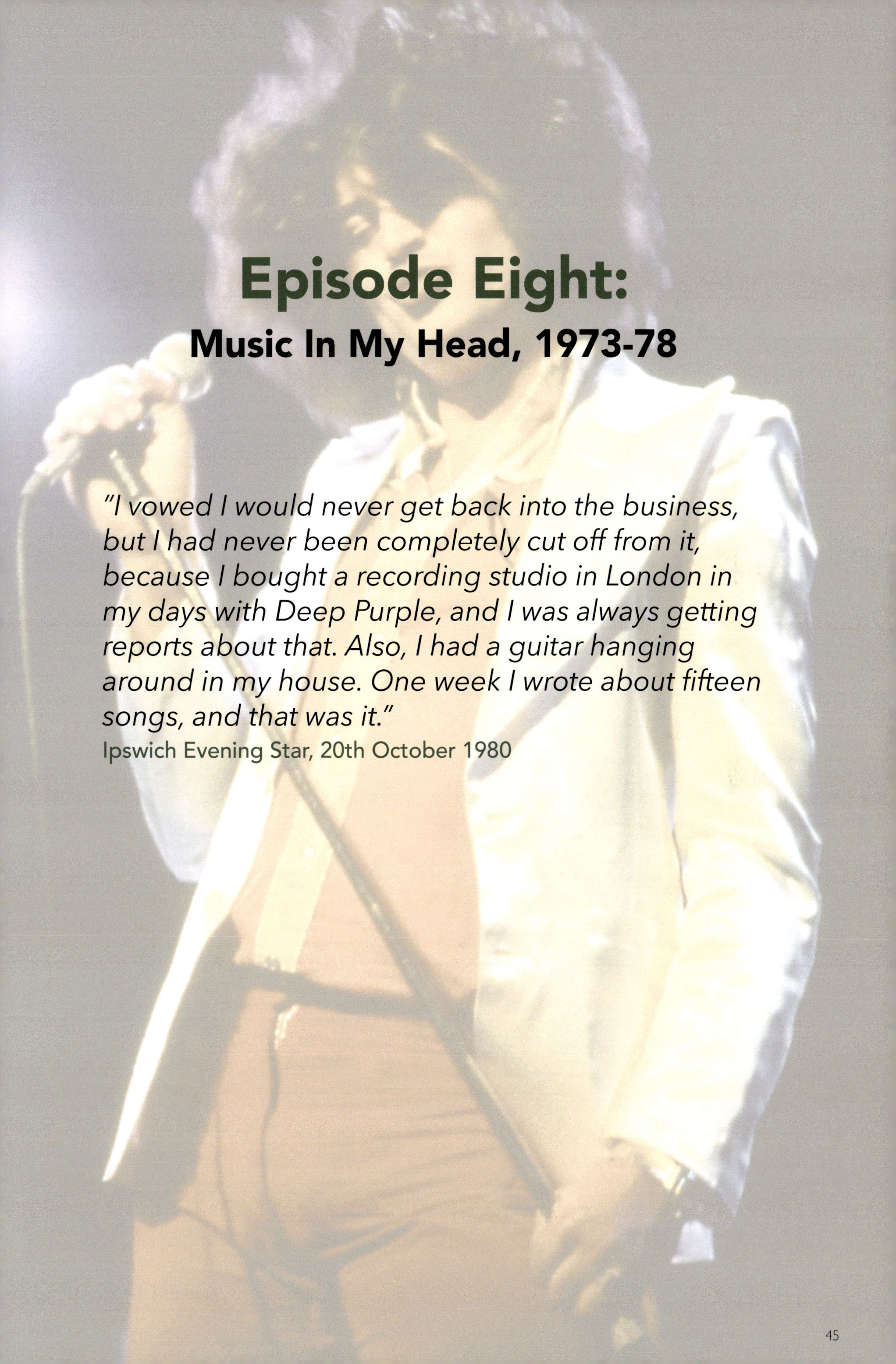

Episode Eight:
Music In My Head, 1973-78

"I vowed I would never get back into the business, but I had never been completely cut off from it, because I bought a recording studio in London in my days with Deep Purple, and I was always getting reports about that. Also, I had a guitar hanging around in my house. One week I wrote about fifteen songs, and that was it."

Ipswich Evening Star, 20th October 1980

Having walked away from Deep Purple in June '73, Ian initially focused his attentions outside of music. With the money accrued he invested in businesses. Most notably the purchase of De Lane Lea Studios on Kingsway in London, which he suitably renamed Kingsway Recorders. But he also invested in a motorcycle engine development project and the purchase of a hotel that was extensively refurbished.

By the spring of '74, less than a year after his break from Purple, Ian went back into the studio to record songs for a debut solo album. The collection of songs showed the diversity of his musical interests, with a couple of 1950s covers including a homage to his teen idol Elvis Presley with 'Tryin' To Get To You'. Self-written songs such as 'Music In My Head' and 'You Led My Heart Astray' were gentle ballads; 'She Called Me Softly', a country style song and only 'You Make Me Feel So Good' was anywhere remotely like anything by Deep Purple.

Unfortunately for Ian, still under the management of Deep Purple's company HEC Enterprises, the album was scrapped. Manager Tony Edwards thought it was too much of a radical departure from what fans would expect.

If Ian was already disillusioned with the music business this rejection of his songs didn't help matters and he continued out of the public eye for the next eighteen months or so. It was Roger Glover who coaxed him back to the stage to sing at the one-off performance of his *Butterfly Ball* album at London's Royal Albert Hall in October '75.

But before he took to the stage Ian was already working on music that would eventually emerge as the debut Ian Gillan Band album, *Child In Time*. Although it included a reworking of the Deep Purple classic and the album title was clearly a way of drawing in the old fans, following on from the recordings the previous year, it was still apparent that Ian wanted to explore different musical ground to that of Purple.

The two albums that followed, in particular *Clear Air Turbulence*, explored even more musical paths but sadly, outside of Japan the audiences showed little appetite for it. Soon Ian took stock of the situation and for his next venture he went back to his roots.

Gillan band

IAN GILLAN, former Deep Purple vocalist, has announced his return from the motorbike showrooms to the rock stage with a hot-shot new band.

The working title which could well be changed (and maybe could do with it!) is Gillan's Shand Grenade.

The line-up is Johnny Gustafson (ex-Roxy, bass and vocals), Mark Nauseef (ex-Elf and Rainbow, percussions), Mike Norman (keyboards) and Ray Fenwick (lead guitar) with Gillan singing and writing most of the material.

The band are going into the studios in January to record an album for release to coincide with a projected March tour of the UK. They begin rehearsals for their live show in Paris at the end of January.

Meanwhile the existence of a 'Deep Purple Live In France' album has been confirmed. The suggestion that Richie Blackmore's refusal to help with overdubs was delaying its release was denied by Purple Music who say that there are no problems, it will be released but that "the time is not right."

Kokomo tour

KOKOMO WILL undertake a full-scale UK tour in February though no dates have so far been confirmed. Last week they augmented their 'official' gig list with three dates at London pub venues.

Ian Gillan circa 76

At the time that Ian was starting to get back into the music business he was looking more like a businessman than a rock star.

Gillan's return

"TO START right at the beginning, I needed a rest when I left Deep Purple. I produced a band called Pussy for a while but after that I just drifted into wilderness, I did nothing, not even listen to the radio." The quote comes from Ian Gillan, the one-time lead vocalist for the English band (he preceded David Coverdale and succeeded Rod Evans). Just about ten months ago he began to feel 're-energized' and after writing several songs entered his own studio to record them. Gillan hired some musicians to perform the material but finding it too multi-directional and confused (from ballads to Tamla) aborted the project.

The turning point was when Ian summoned former Purple bassist Roger Glover to produce him; Gillan found another group of players and after successful sessions in Munich decided to keep the musicians and use them in the studio and on the road. With material already written during those preliminary sessions in Germany, the album was recorded at the beginning of January. The band includes Ray Fenwich on guitar (formerly with Spencer Davis), Joe Gustavson on bass and vocals, Mike Moran on keyboards, and Mark Nausseef on drums and percussion (formerly with Elf).

"What we're doing is music which is played well by great players and it's 'now' sort of music." says Gillan. "And lyrically and vocally it's what I always have been and that's just a plain rock singer.

"And to be fair I'd have to say there is a resemblance to Deep Purple when I was in the band if for the only reason that it's the same voice, the same singer."

The band takes to the road in March ("They won't be as loud as Purple was") while the album will be released in mid-February (containing one previous Purple track from 'In Rock' titled 'Child In Time'). Gillan cites this as a link from the past to the present and it contains some of his most adventurous vocal work while with Purple.

"I was becoming stagnant and we (Purple) became so entrenched in parallel lines that we dared not pass because that was the Purple identity and image, that we were really restricting our means of expression."

— Steve Rosen.

Oyster IAN GILLAN BAND

The Ian Gillan Band, or IGB as it was quickly referred as surprised many fans with its musical style and was a far cry from Deep Purple.

Bilzen 77

Eight years on from playing the Bilzen Festival with Purple, Ian returned to it with his own band on 13th August 1977.

The Japanese tour in September '77 was a triumphant return for Ian to the country where he had played his last shows with Deep Purple.

Enjoying some relaxation in the Kyoto Gardens.

UDO ARTISTS, INC.
KYODO BLDG. 5-9-15
MINAMI-AOYAMA MINATO-KU,
TOKYO JAPAN
CABLE ADDRESS: UDOARTISTSPRO TOKYO
TEL-400-6 5 3 6~8

TELEX: J26552 (UDOART)

I T I N E R A R Y

IAN GILLAN BAND　　　＊＊＊＊＊＊　GROUP (1)　＊＊＊＊＊＊　MEMBERS

Sept 9	Fri		Arrive Tokyo by
			Check in Ginza Tokyu Hotel (Tel: 541-2411)
10	Sat		Rehearsal (?)
11	Sun	11:30 AM	Baggage down
		12:00 Noon	Check out of Ginza Tokyu Hotel, proceed to Tokyo Airport
		1:40 PM	Leave Tokyo for Osaka by All Nippon Airways #27
		2:35 PM	Arrive Osaka
			Check in Osaka Grand Hotel (Tel: 202-1212)
12	Mon	1:45 PM	Leave hotel, proceed to Osaka Kosei Nenkin Hall
		2:00 PM	Rehearsal
		5:45 PM	Doors open
		6:30 PM	Concert at OSAKA KOSEI NENKIN HALL
13	Tue	4:00 PM	Leave hotel, proceed to Osaka Kosei Nenkin Hall
		4:15 PM	Sound check
		5:45 PM	Doors open
		6:30 PM	Concert at OSAKA KOSEI NENKIN HALL
14	Wed	12:00 Noon	Baggage down
		12:30 PM	Check out of Osaka Grand Hotel, proceed to Kyoto by car (1½ hour drive)
		2:00 PM	Check in Kyoto Grand Hotel (Tel: 341-2311)
		4:00 PM	Leave hotel, proceed to Kyoto Kaikan Hall
		4:30 PM	Sound check
		5:45 PM	Doors open
		6:30 PM	Concert at KYOTO KAIKAN DAI-ICHI HALL
15	Thu		Day Off
		10:00 PM	Baggage down
16	Fri	11:30 AM	Check out of Kyoto Grand Hotel, proceed to Kyoto Station
		11:53 AM	Leave Kyoto for Hiroshima by Super Express "Hikari" #23
		2:08 PM	Arrive Hiroshima
			Check in Hiroshima Grand Hotel (Tel: 27-1313)
		4:15 PM	Leave hotel, proceed to Hiroshima Yubin Chokin Hall
		4:30 PM	Sound check
		5:45 PM	Doors open
		6:30 PM	Concert at HIROSHIMA YUBIN CHOKIN HALL
		10:30 PM	Baggage down

HOTEL INFORMATIONS

Sept 10	GINZA TOKYU HOTEL	5-15-9 Ginza, Chuo-ku, Tokyo Tel: (03) 541-2411
Sept 11 - 14	OSAKA GRAND HOTEL	2-22 Naka-no-Shima, Kita-ku Osaka City Tel: (06) 202-1212
Sept 15 - 16	HIROSHIMA GRAND HOTEL	4-4 Kami Hatcho-Bori Hiroshima City Tel: (0822) 27-1313
Sept 17	NISHI-TETSU GRAND HOTEL	2-6-60 Daimyo, Chuo-ku, Fukuoka City Tel: (092) 771-7171
Sept 18 - 22	GINZA TOKYU HOTEL	

```
IAN GILLAN BAND   GROUP (1) / PAGE 2

Sept 17  Sat   11:30 AM   Check out of Hirohsima Grand Hotel, proceed to
                          Hiroshima Station
               12:10 AM   Leave Hiroshima for Fukuoka by Super Express "Hikari" #1
                1:56 PM   Arrive Hakata, Fukuoka
                          Check in Nishi-Tetsu Grand Hotel (Tel: 771-7171)
                4:15 PM   Leave hotel, proceed to Kyuden Taiiku-Kan
                4:30 PM   Sound check
                5:45 PM   Doors open
                6:30 PM   Concert at KYUDEN TAIIKU-KAN

        18 Sun 12:30 PM   Baggage down
                1:00 PM   Check out of Nishi-Tetsu Grand Hotel, proceed to
                          Fukuoka Airport
                2:30 PM   Leave Fukuoka for Tokyo by All Nippon Airways #252
                4:00 PM   Arrive Tokyo
                          Check in Ginza Tokyu Hotel (Tel: 541-2411)

        19 Mon            Day Off

        20 Tue            Day Off

        21 Wed            Day Off

        22 Thu  3:45 PM   Leave hotel, proceed to Budokan
                4:15 PM   Sound check
                5:30 PM   Doors open
                6:30 PM   Concert at BUDOKAN

        23 Fri            Leave Japan
```

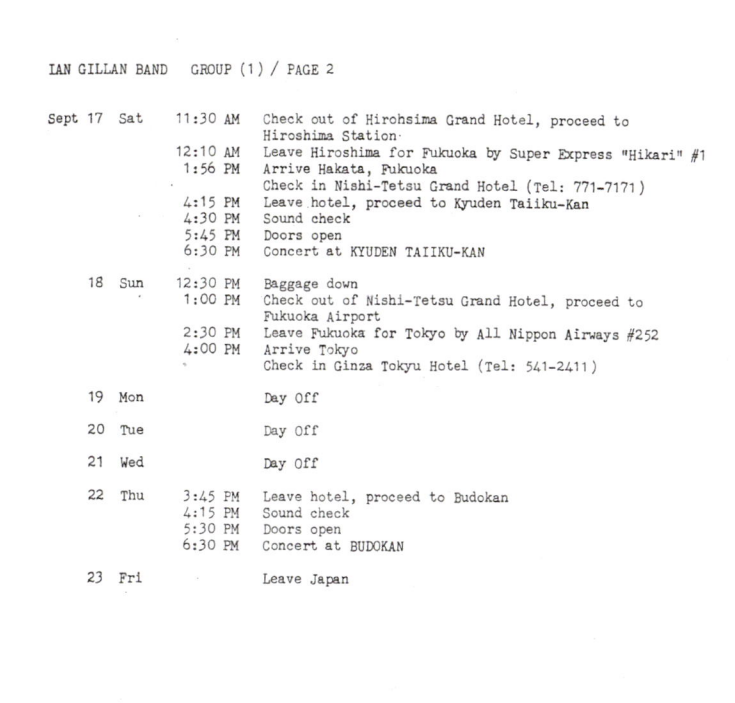

© Ray Fenwick

© Ray Fenwick

© Ray Fenwick

Backstage in Tokyo.

© Ray Fenwick

© Ray Fenwick

Towards the end of IGB. The fancy clothes would give way to a more rock 'n' roll look with the next band.

Episode Nine:
Secret Of The Dance, 1978-82

"That just ran its course like everything does. I knew I wanted to do something different but wasn`t sure what I was going to end up with but I knew I wanted something that was a little more direct and much less complicated. I didn`t have the courage to fire the guys so I left my own band and started another one and we got Mick Underwood involved and John McCoy turned up at the studio one day and it went from there. I don`t really know how he ended up in the band but he looked great and played in exactly the style that I was after that was very direct, powerful and uncomplicated. Colin stayed with us and with Bernie there as our new banjo player who had such immense talent and personality and Bob`s your Uncle we had a new band. That`s how it went. We all just seemed to work so well together."

Interview with Mick Burgess, 25th September 2016

After two and a half years and three albums, the Ian Gillan Band had reached the end of the line. The sophisticated style hadn't sat well with many of Ian's traditional fans and he wanted to get back to rock 'n' roll with a revamped band, simply called Gillan.

Whilst it would prove to be a smart commercial move, initially it was a very difficult period. The recording contract with Chris Blackwell's Island Records was over and with Disco, Punk and New Wave dominating the UK music scene, traditional rock was struggling to find a foothold.

The debut *Gillan* album initially only saw release on EMI's Eastworld label in Japan, who also subsequently licensed it to Australia and New Zealand. But within a year, a UK record deal had been secured and with the *Mr Universe* album Gillan reached number 11 in the UK album charts. Ian Gillan was back in the game.

There was a hiccup when the initial success looked like it might flounder as the UK record company Acrobat went bust. Fortunately, Richard Branson signed Gillan to Virgin Records and even greater success ensued.

Four albums followed, all hitting the UK top 20 and several hit singles as well, that also saw Gillan appear on the UK's flagship music show Top Of The Pops on numerous occasions between 1980-82.

Sadly, as the band set out in 1982 to tour in promotion of the *Magic* album it was clearly apparent that Ian was struggling with his voice and under medical advice, he had to take time off. Behind the scenes band members were also unhappy with the financials and Gillan finished in a rather unpleasant way following the show at Wembley Arena on 17th December 1982.

After surgery and recuperation, when Ian re-emerged in mid-1983 the career move he made came as a surprise to most.

Ian relaxing at his Kingsway Recorders studio in London. It was around this time that he took stock of his direction and re-launched himself with a new band simply called Gillan. It reflected the more straightforward rock 'n' roll approach that Ian thought was necessary.

The debut performance for the new band was at the 1978 Reading Festival. Although the press adverts billed them as the Ian Gillan Band, this was Gillan. With a revamped band they did a short set consisting of 'Secret Of The Dance,' 'Back In The Game,' 'Child In Time,' 'Dead Of Night,' 'Message In A Bottle,' 'Smoke On The Water' and 'Lucille'. Aside from the two Purple songs and Little Richard's 'Lucille', the rest of the set was new songs that had only just been recorded and would initially only be released in Japan the following month.

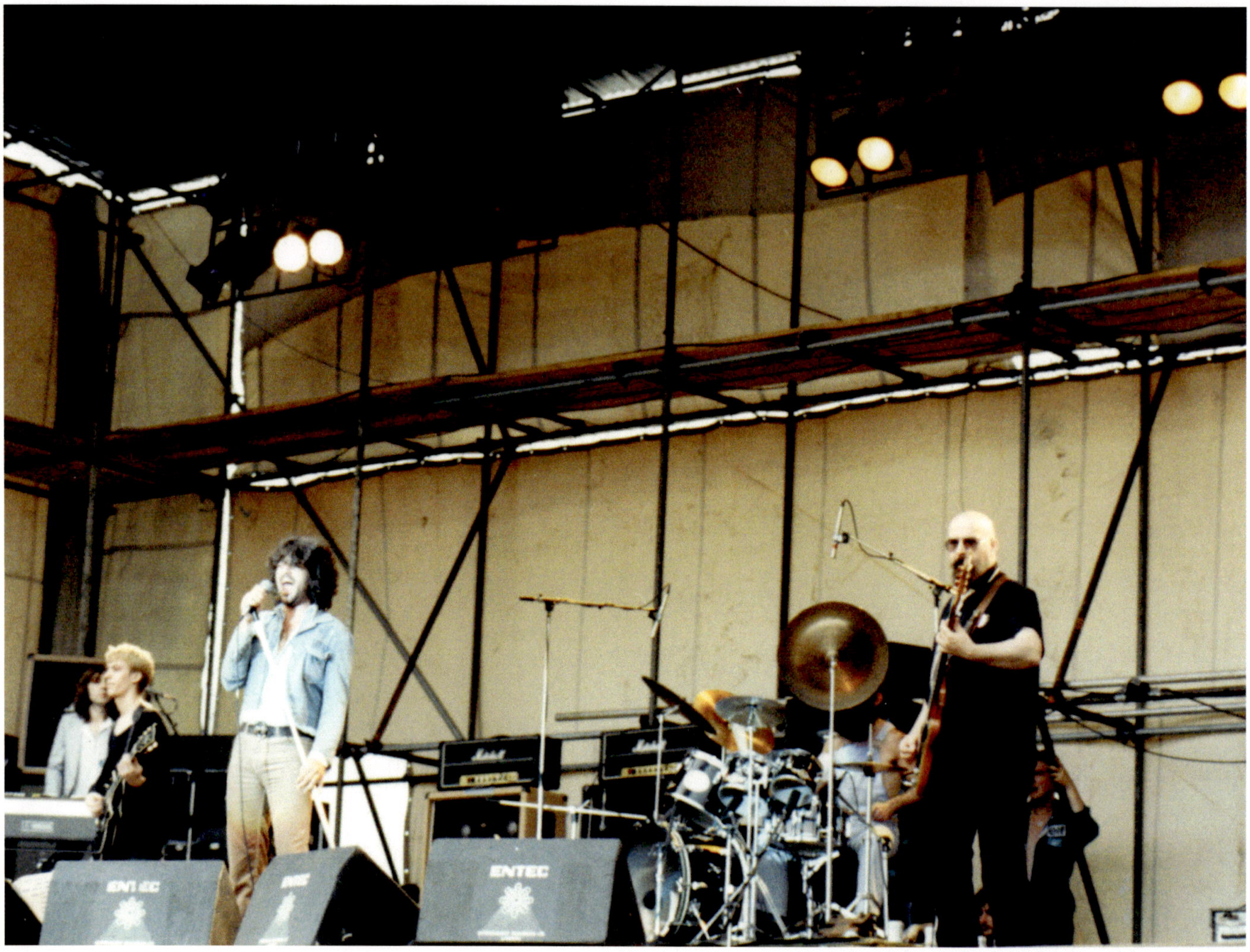
ENTEC

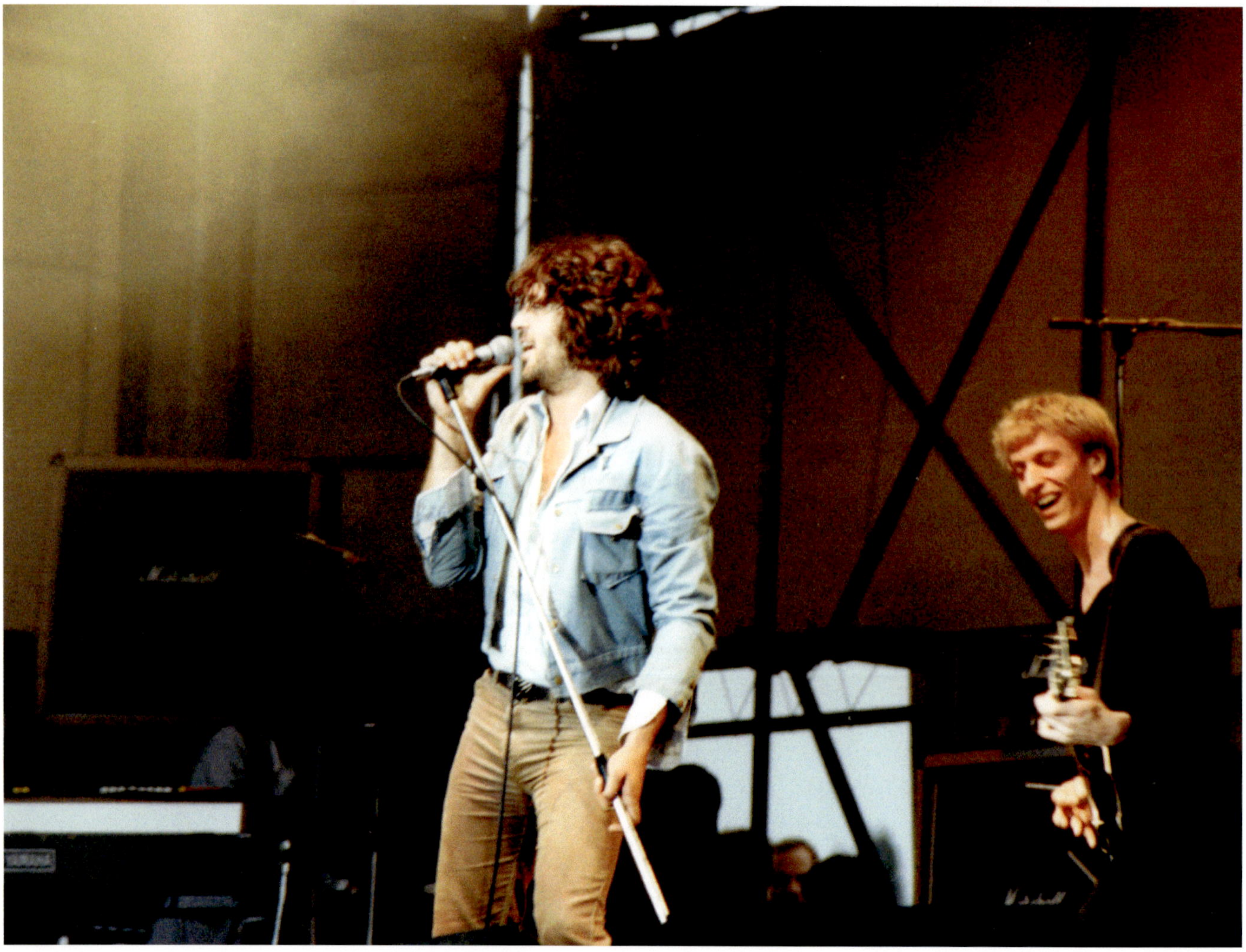

Bruinisse Bru Pop Open Air Festival, Holland, 11th August 1979

Open air festivals proved to be a good way to introduce new fans to the new Gillan sound as Ian re-built his career as the eighties arrived.

Ian would play guitar for the rock 'n' roll encores.

Genk Limburg Hall, Belgium, 29th May 1981

During the soundcheck

© Marc Brans

© Marc Brans

© Marc Brans

© Marc Brans

67

Poperinge, Belgium 29th January 1982

Back in Genk, 30th January 1982 with new guitarist Janick Gers in tow.

© Marc Brans

© Mick Gregory

© Mick Gregory

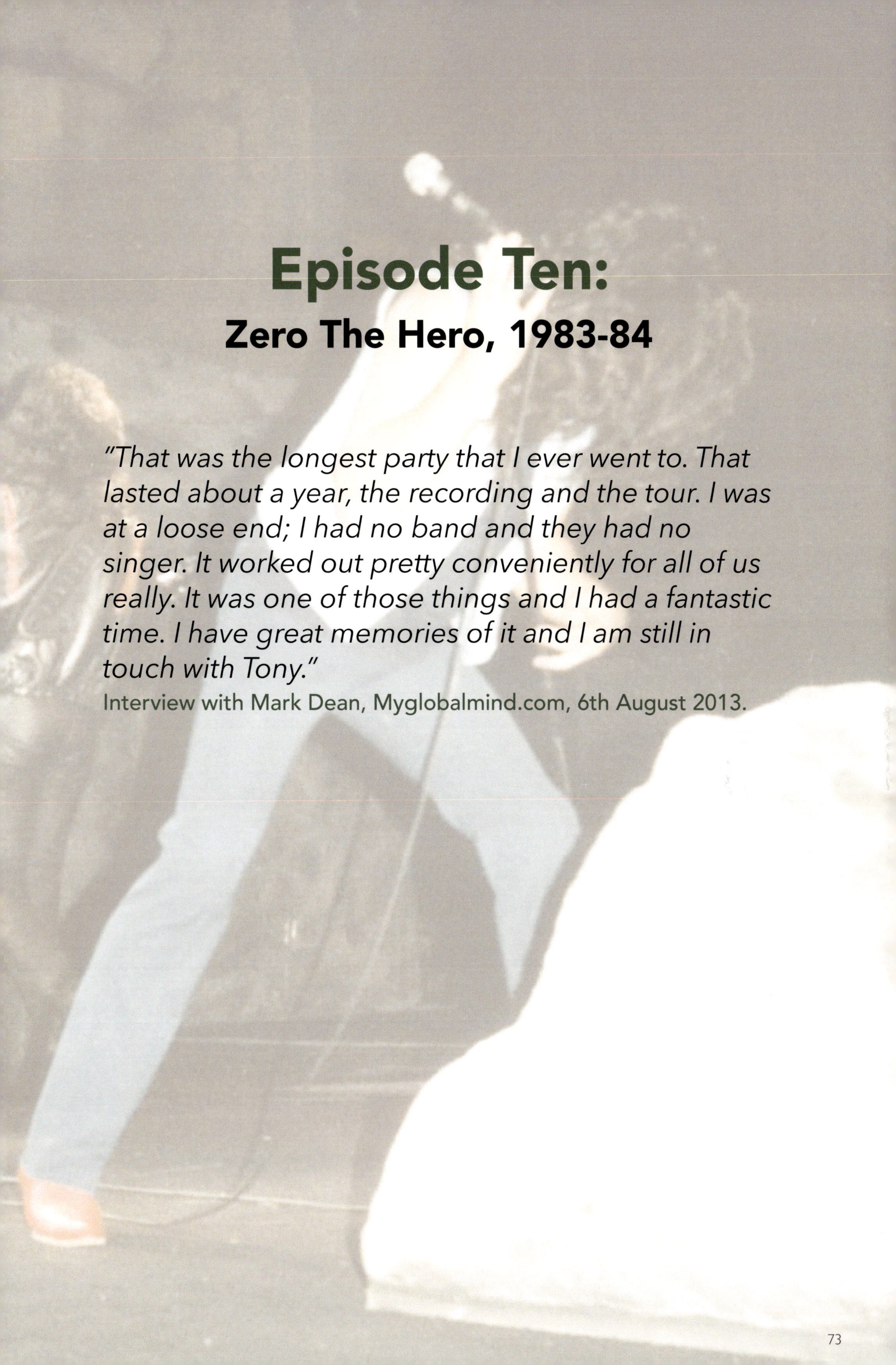

Episode Ten:
Zero The Hero, 1983-84

"That was the longest party that I ever went to. That lasted about a year, the recording and the tour. I was at a loose end; I had no band and they had no singer. It worked out pretty conveniently for all of us really. It was one of those things and I had a fantastic time. I have great memories of it and I am still in touch with Tony."
Interview with Mark Dean, Myglobalmind.com, 6th August 2013.

Ian has repeatedly said that his decision to join Black Sabbath was as a result of one very long drinking session in the Bear in Oxford with Tony Iommi and Geezer Butler. As poetic as the story might be, it's highly unlikely that any contracts were signed until Ian was sober.

Indeed, the break up of Gillan, had as much to do with Ian's desire to get Deep Purple back together again but when the initial discussions concerning that were put on hold, taking on the role of Black Sabbath's lead singer at least helped to re-establish Ian's name in the States. Neither IGB or Gillan had attained any measurable level of recognition in America and it was now ten years on since he quit Purple. Ian had simply not registered on the consciences of most American rock fans in the decade since.

Recorded at Richard Branson's Manor Studio in Oxfordshire in May '83, Black Sabbath's *Born Again* was released in August. Extensive touring commenced in Europe the same month. The band spent October through to early March '84 touring the big arenas in North America but behind the scenes the Deep Purple reunion was building momentum.

Ian did his last show with Black Sabbath on 4th March 1984 at the Civic Centre, Springfield Massachusetts. The following month another episode in Ian's life began.

The teaming up with Black Sabbath caught most people unaware. After the album was completed former ELO drummer Bev Bevan was brought in to replace the incapacitated Bill Ward and along with Geezer Butler and Tony Iommi, six months of touring, mainly in North America, commenced.

Forest National, Brussels, 1st October 1983

© Marc Brans

Ian has spoken many times about his struggle to remember the words to the older Sabbath songs, prompting him to use cue sheets to read them from.

Relaxing backstage after the show.

Episode Eleven:
Back In The Game, 1984-89

"It was very strange, you know. It was getting together, like a school reunion. Everyone was very polite, and 'what have you been doing?', nice conversations. We didn't know if it was going to work because, of course, we all had changed and had other experiences. It was generally very nice, everyone was very polite, we were locked away in a big house in Vermont, in North America in the wintertime. We lit the fire, came down to the basement and started jamming. And you could see in couple of minutes everyone smiling and thinking 'yeah, yeah, it's gonna be okay'. That's what I remember."
Wikimetal, 29th November 2011

The much talked about and for many, wished for Deep Purple reunion finally happened eleven years on from Ian's departure in 1973. Whilst Purple had of course carried on for another three years, the classic MkII line-up was always considered the defining representation of the name Deep Purple. For most fans, the 1984 album *Perfect Strangers* gave a feeling of the band having never been away and the ensuing tour was a box office smash. Everything was back to normal… for a while anyway.

By 1987 a second album *The House Of Blue Light* wasn't received as positively although the world tour to promote it continued to see the band filling arenas. Unfortunately Ian's relationship with Ritchie Blackmore, that had been instrumental in the split first time around was brewing up again. By 1989, Ian found himself at a loose end as the rest of Deep Purple gave him the "Spanish Archer".

Time to unleash the naked thunder…

DEEP PURPLE BLAST BACK
Ten-million dollar men

★ DEEP PURPLE, Britain's best heavy metal band before they split in the early Seventies, are back with their original line-up.

And I can exclusively reveal that they have celebrated the reunion by signing a 10-million dollar deal with the Polygram record company.

The massive contract is to do just four LPs—the first of which, Perfect Strangers, is being completed in Hamburg for November release.

Ian Gillan, Jon Lord, Ian Paice, Richie Blackmore and Roger Glover were the best-known incarnation of Purple.

Famed for classics like Smoke on the Water and Black Night, they had a very combustible relationship before they split in 1973.

Although the band continued with Whitesnake's David Coverdale on vocals, true fans claim they were never the same again.

Now that they are reunited, they are planning a worldwide series of concerts ending in Britain next April.

Guitarist Richie Blackmore—a noted weirdo with an interest in the occult—is going to relax in a strange manner before starting the tour rehearsals. He is going ghost hunting in Germany for two days.

Will this provide inspiration for a hit single?

REUNITED: (from left) Paice, Blackmore, Gillan, Lord and Glover.

79

Deep Purple to tune up Down Under

HEAVY metal heroes *Deep Purple*, who announced their reformation in Hamburg last week, have revealed that their comeback world tour will begin in Australia.

Ian Gillan, Ian Paice, Roger Glover, Jon Lord and *Ritchie Blackmore* loved Australia when they toured way back in May 1971.

And that's the line-up that will be making the return, despite two of its members being involved in other heavy metal bands — Gillan with a band that bears his name and Blackmore with *Rainbow*.

The guys decided to make Australia their starting point after talking with the likes of *Elton John* and *Rod Stewart* who have proved time and time again that Down Under audiences don't lack enthusiasm.

Deep Purple stormed through the rock scene in the late 1960s and early '70s, rivalled only by *Led Zeppelin*. Their hits included *My Woman From Tokyo*, *Black Night* and the classic *Smoke On The Water*.

© Mick Gregory

PITTSBURGH — They may be "old" by heavy metal standards, but their music still blisters with youthful fire.

They are Deep Purple, bassist Roger Glover, guitarist Ritchie Blackmore, singer Ian Gillan, keyboardist Jon Lord and drummer Ian Paice, one of the pioneering bands of rock's heavy metal genre.

Last night, they issued an effective reminder before a sold out Civic Arena audience that rock 'n' roll is not about chronological age, but about spirit and feeling.

Concert review

Rex Rutkoski

Valley News Dispatch

Heavy metal primarily is the turf of the very young rock 'n' rollers. But it didn't lose a beat when translated yesterday by these five musicians who all are hovering near the age of 40.

The enthusiastic box office response to the reunion of Deep Purple's most popular and strongest lineup may be the surprise of '85 in the entertainment industry.

The Pittsburgh show, for example, sold out within a few days and there was an attempt to add a second concert, but the dates did not coincide with Deep Purple's tour routing.

Judging from the generally youthful audience, it would not be surprising if many in the crowd, estimated at 12,500, viewed the show as an opportunity to experience some rock history.

For them, that history likely began, not with the '50s, but in the early '70s era of Deep Purple's "Machine Head" album, which produced their trademark "Smoke On The Water."

Though formed in 1968, Deep Purple seems quite comfortable in 1985.

They wedded two eras of heavy metal in yesterday's show, taking advantage of sound and lighting technology not available to them in their last appearance in Pittsburgh many years ago.

Lasers, colorful overhead lighting and rear screen projections added a forcefulness to their presentation, making even their classics new again.

The evening began with a warmup set of basic hard rock from the band Giuffria.

After a long intermission, Deep Purple opened on a high note with "Highway Star," Gillan's powerful voice and Blackmore's searing guitar riffs in tasty complement.

The band, though, did not rely on their oldies to establish the early part of the program. After "Highway Star," they reeled-off about a half dozen songs from their new "Perfect Strangers" album before dipping back to 1969 for "Child In Time," a wonderful showcase of changing musical emotions.

About 30 minutes into the set, there was some confusion when the band seemed to end the "Perfect Strangers" title track abruptly, Gillan raised five fingers and the musicians left the stage.

The audience, apparently not understanding that there was a power failure with the band's equipment and that Gillan was giving a "take five" signal, roared for more music.

The problem was solved within minutes, and Deep Purple soon was back to draining the house wattage. "I guess somebody didn't pay the electric bill," Gillan quipped.

The 14-song, one-hour-and-50-minute performance included time to spotlight the individual solo talents of the band. Lord turned the classical composition "Ode To Joy" into a variation of hard rock themes.

"Space Truckin'" closed the regular portion of the concert, and the band was returned for an encore segment.

The first of the encore material was a shortened version of "Woman From Tokyo," with the band sending huge beach balloons into the crowd.

"Smoke On The Water," was the finale, and, though almost a decade and a half old, it did not sound dated.

Limburghall, Genk, Belgium, 24th June 1985

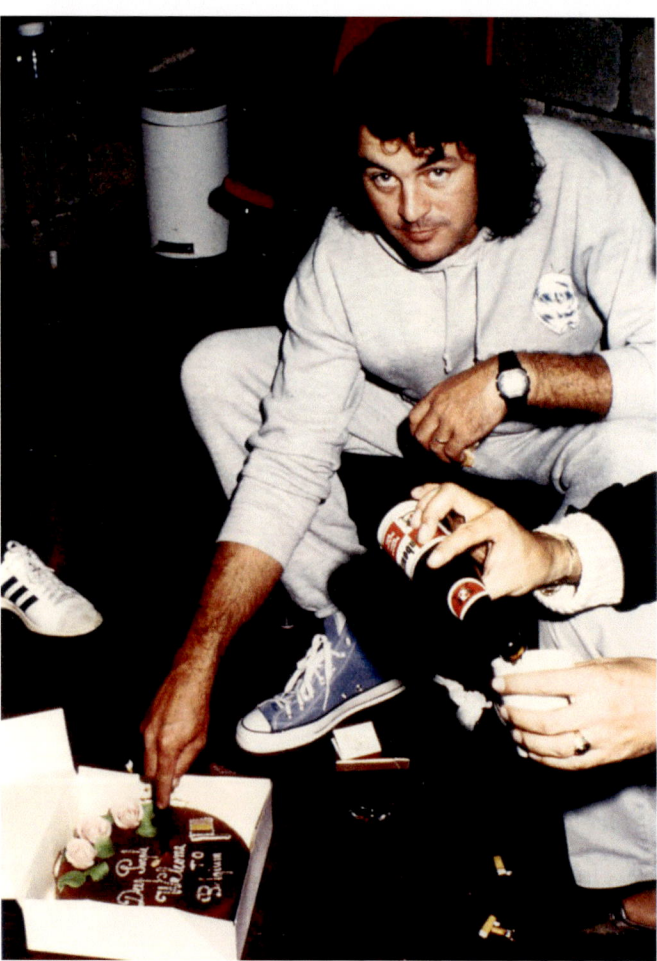

Enjoying a cake prepared specially for Purple's visit to Belgium. The first time the MKII line-up had played there since March 1973.

Press conference in Cologne, Germany, February 1987.

Olympiahalle, Munich, 17th February 1987

Although the second reunion tour was also very successful, the relationship with Blackmore was starting to breakdown again.

East Rutherford, Giants Stadium - New Jersey, USA, 16th August 1988

This huge show saw the band headline on a bill with Aerosmith and Guns N' Roses but it was one of only two US shows that year. A short European tour followed but Ian soon found himself kicked out of the band as frictions rose.

With Jim Marshall, founder of Marshall Amplification at a private function in London in 1988.

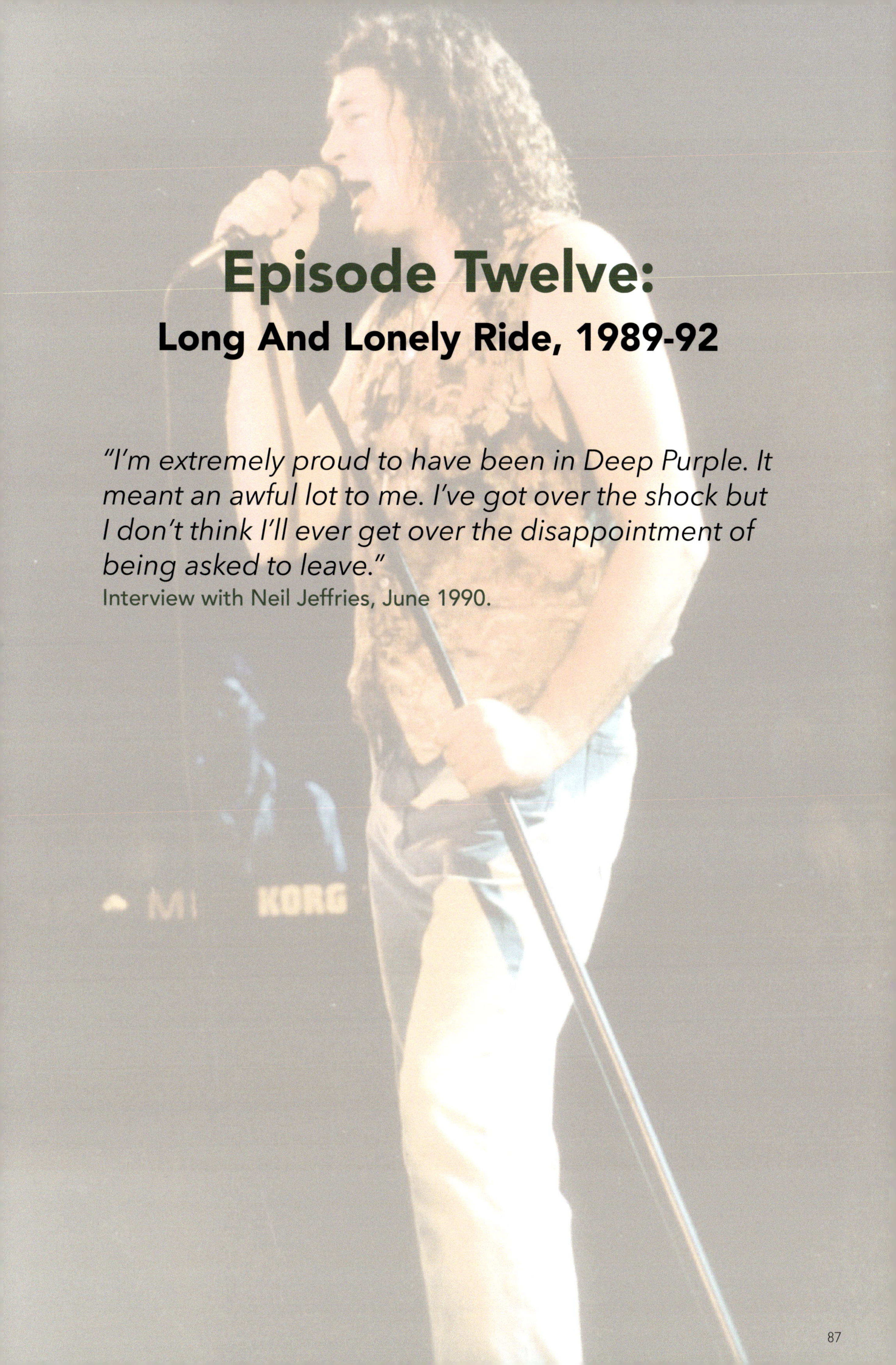

Episode Twelve:
Long And Lonely Ride, 1989-92

"I'm extremely proud to have been in Deep Purple. It meant an awful lot to me. I've got over the shock but I don't think I'll ever get over the disappointment of being asked to leave."
Interview with Neil Jeffries, June 1990.

Ian has always been philosophical about his career taking the rough with the smooth. His insatiable desire to write and perform simply meant that whether or not Deep Purple wanted him, there was plenty more he could offer his fans.

Ian teamed up with guitarist and songwriter Steve Morris from the Liverpool based band Export for 1990's *Naked Thunder* album. The supporting cast included former Quatermass keyboard player Peter Robinson and top session drummer Simon Phillips. The assembled live band to support it included the rhythm section from The Sensational Alex Harvey Band – Ted McKenna and Chris Glenn.

The next album *Toolbox* was credited as Gillan and used the logo from the eighties band. From 1990-92 Ian toured relentlessly in many far-flung places visiting many countries that he had never played before. From former Soviet Union states, to Venezuela and Bolivia and even the Faroe Islands. Somewhat surprisingly, in mid-92 calls were made for Ian to re-join Deep Purple to celebrate the upcoming 25th anniversary of the band's inception. It seemed improbable and even more so that he would agree. But his "gut reaction" was that he had "nothing to lose".

Ettelbruck Hall Deich, Luxembourg, 16th October 1990

© Marc Brans

© Marc Brans

On the tour bus after the gig and getting ready for bed!

Live Music Hall, Cologne, Germany, 12th November 1991.

1991 saw a second album with *Toolbox* and another tour but soon Ian was getting the call to return to Deep Purple.

Episode Thirteen:
Ramshackle Man, 1992-1994

"I remember clearly saying last year that I would rather slit my throat than ever sing with these guys again and I was going through a very happy phase. I'd been through two years of development with my own band and after last Christmas we'd got a new guitar player and everything was going beautifully. In fact we were in pre-production in Holland doing demos. This was late last year. Everyone assumed I was going to do it and the more I said no, the more it looked as if I was being difficult again or sulking because I'd been fired. So in the end the guys in my band said, 'look you've got to do it. Everyone wants you to do it, give it one hundred per cent and it better be good'. I went out to Germany and there was Jon Lord, and we had a cuddle and that was it and we went out and had a bottle of wine and everything was fine. I don't think we wanted to face those difficulties we'd been through. We just wanted to deal with the thing as it was. Ritchie was there, we had a few beers and a game of football or two."

Interview with Claire Sturgess, Friday Rock Show, 16th July 1993

When Ian agreed to re-join Deep Purple for his third stint fronting the band his initial thoughts were to commit to the twenty-fifth anniversary as a project and when it was all over to return to his own group, which he had re-branded as Repo Depo.

Everyone knew that being on stage with his old adversary Ritchie Blackmore was going to present some challenges as Deep Purple returned to the stage in September 1993. But no one could have foreseen the turn of events that happened. Events that in turn would change Ian's mind.

Undoubtedly Deep Purple experienced a roller coaster of a journey in the early nineties but when the dust had settled, Ian just put his heart back into the band as the next episode of his musical journey began.

Ian in Zurich during a promotional trip for *The Battle Rages On…*

The first night of the German leg of the tour in Schwerin, 1st October 1993.

Opening night of the UK dates at the Apollo, Manchester, 5th November.

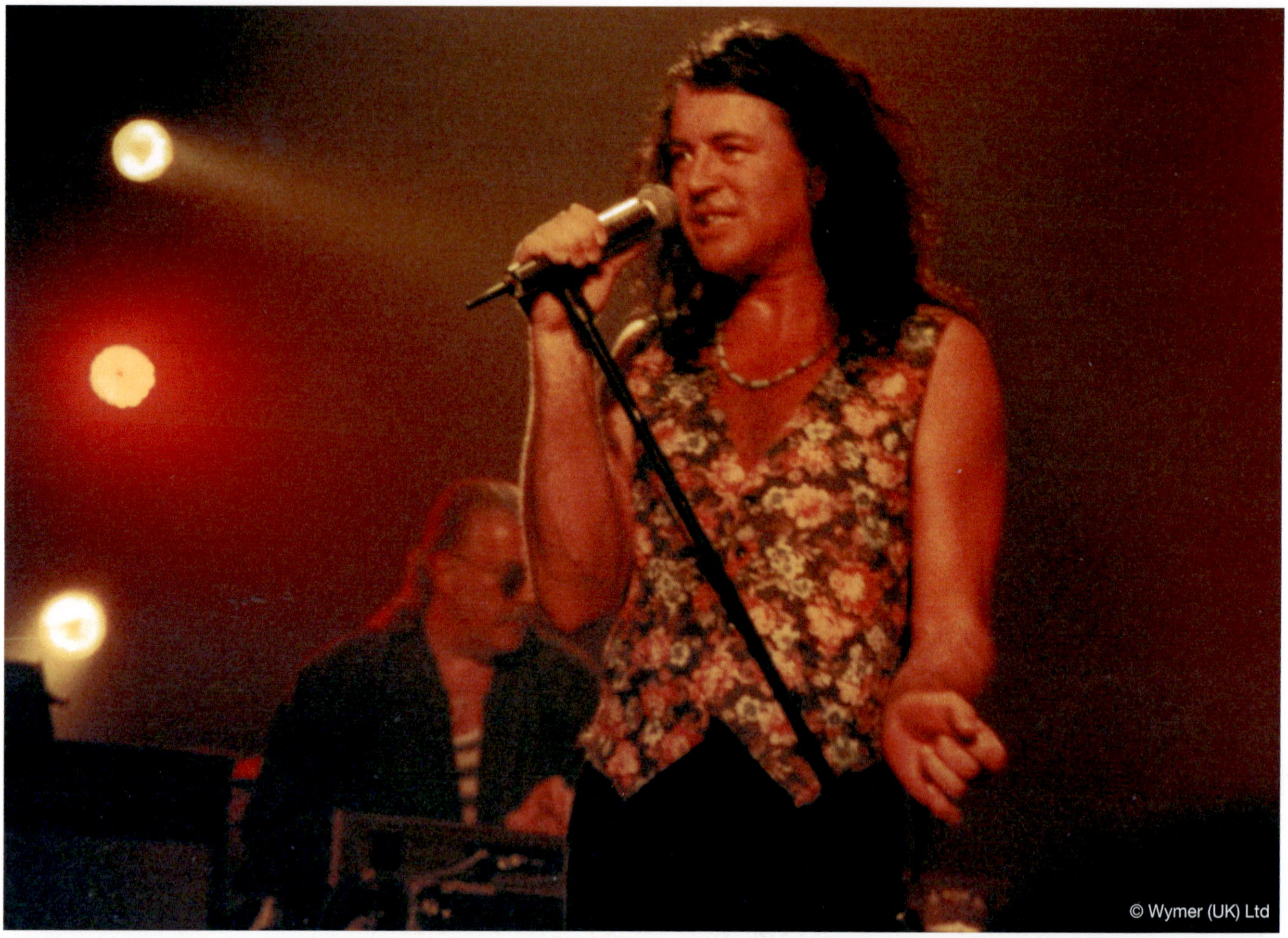
© Wymer (UK) Ltd

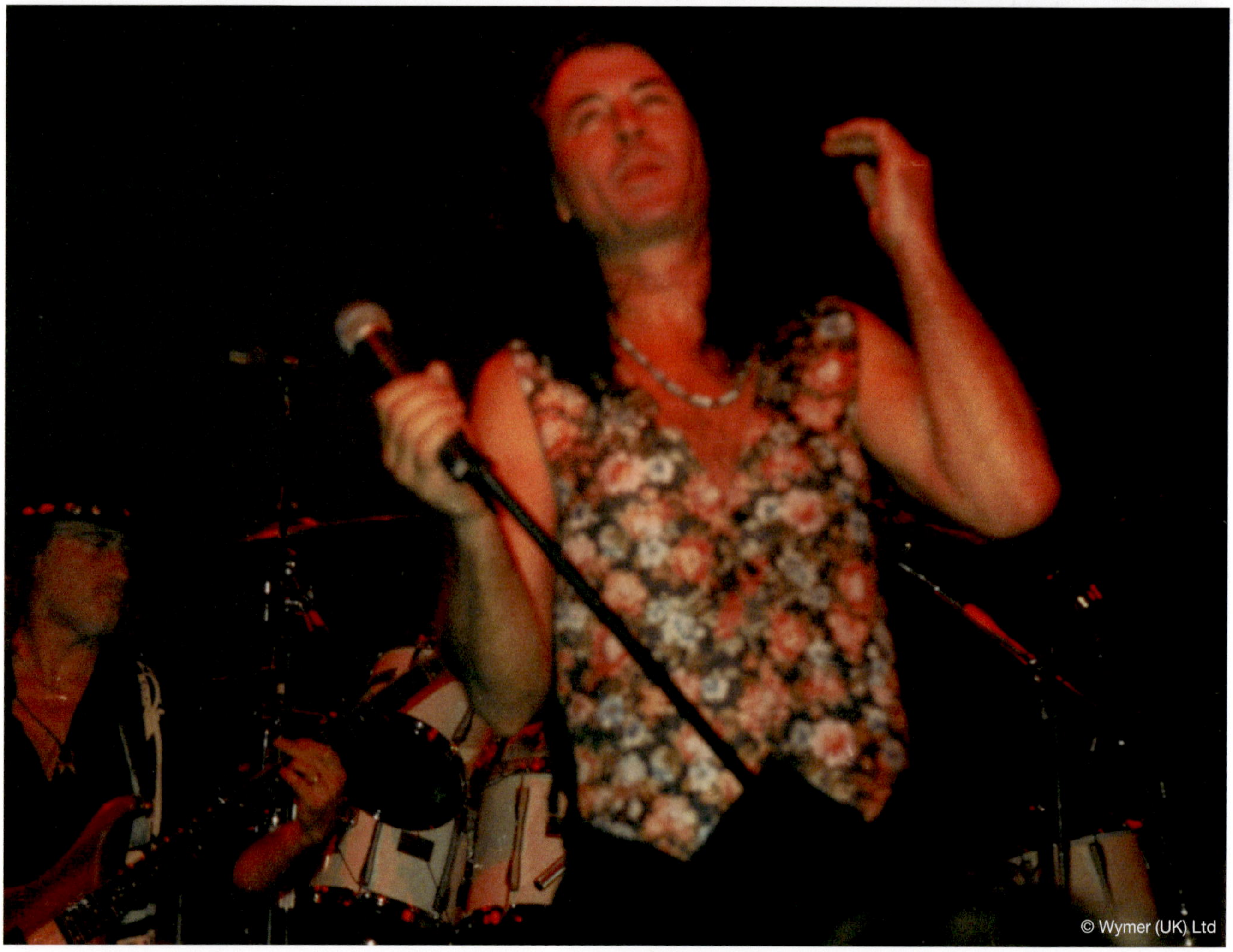
© Wymer (UK) Ltd

NEC, Birmingham, 9th November.

© Rob Reynolds

In all there would only be 37 shows with the classic line-up. By the time of this gig Blackmore had already informed the others he was leaving after the show in Helsinki. Joe Satriani was drafted in to complete the Japanese gigs and stayed for a little while the following year before the next major phase in Purple's illustrious career began.

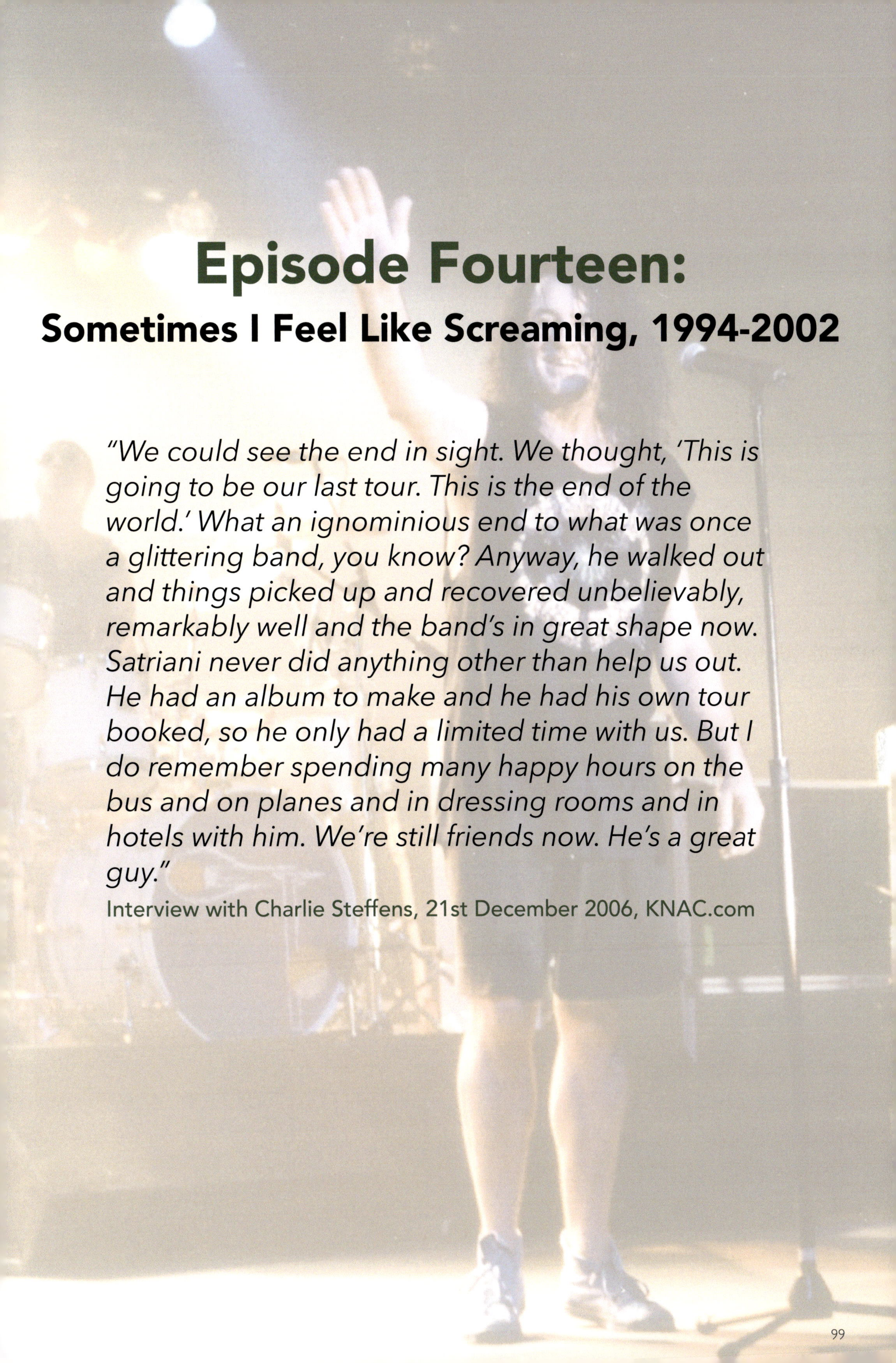

Episode Fourteen:
Sometimes I Feel Like Screaming, 1994-2002

"We could see the end in sight. We thought, 'This is going to be our last tour. This is the end of the world.' What an ignominious end to what was once a glittering band, you know? Anyway, he walked out and things picked up and recovered unbelievably, remarkably well and the band's in great shape now. Satriani never did anything other than help us out. He had an album to make and he had his own tour booked, so he only had a limited time with us. But I do remember spending many happy hours on the bus and on planes and in dressing rooms and in hotels with him. We're still friends now. He's a great guy."

Interview with Charlie Steffens, 21st December 2006, KNAC.com

Having got over the drama of 1993 Deep Purple entered a new era with guitarist Steve Morse that has turned out to be the most stable in the band's incredibly enduring career.

It was a period that also saw the band embark on a heavier touring schedule that took them to countries that Purple had never performed in before. Places such as South Korea, South Africa and India and even managing to create two new albums. They also toured Australia for the first time in fifteen years and documented it on film.

1999 saw the thirtieth anniversary of Jon Lord's *Concerto For Group & Orchestra* celebrated with a brace of gigs at the Royal Albert Hall. 2000 saw the band's most ambitious tour schedule as they took orchestras on the road in South America and Europe to give thousands more the chance to hear the Concerto performed.

Whilst it fulfilled a personal ambition for Jon Lord, the following year he had to step down with a knee problem and former Rainbow keyboard player Don Airey stepped in. By 2002 Airey had taken over permanently as Lord no longer wished to commit to the level of touring that the band was now geared to. The next episode was upon Ian, only this time it would continue "infinite".

Flanders Expo, Gent, 18th June 1994.

© Marc Brans

Same waistcoat, different guitarist. Following the Japanese shows, Satriani did one European tour through June and July but his other commitments meant that Purple had to look for a new guitarist as they prepared for the future

Relaxing off stage in Gent.

Brabanthallen, 's-Hertogenbosch, Netherlands, 24th June 1994.

Different waistcoat for the only Dutch show with Satriani.

Back at the hotel after the gig.

At the very first press conference at the Presidente Hotel in Mexico City on 23rd November 1994, presenting new guitarist Steve Morse to the band.

At the Sports Palace in Mexico City in 23rd November 1994. The very first show with (out of shot) Morse.

Brielpoort, Deinze, 6th October 1996

Forest Vorst National, Brussels, 24th September 1998

Sportpaleis, Antwerpen, 30th September 2000 performing the "Concerto" along with a mix of other material. The tour included Ronnie James Dio who would join Ian at the end of the show for 'Smoke On The Water'

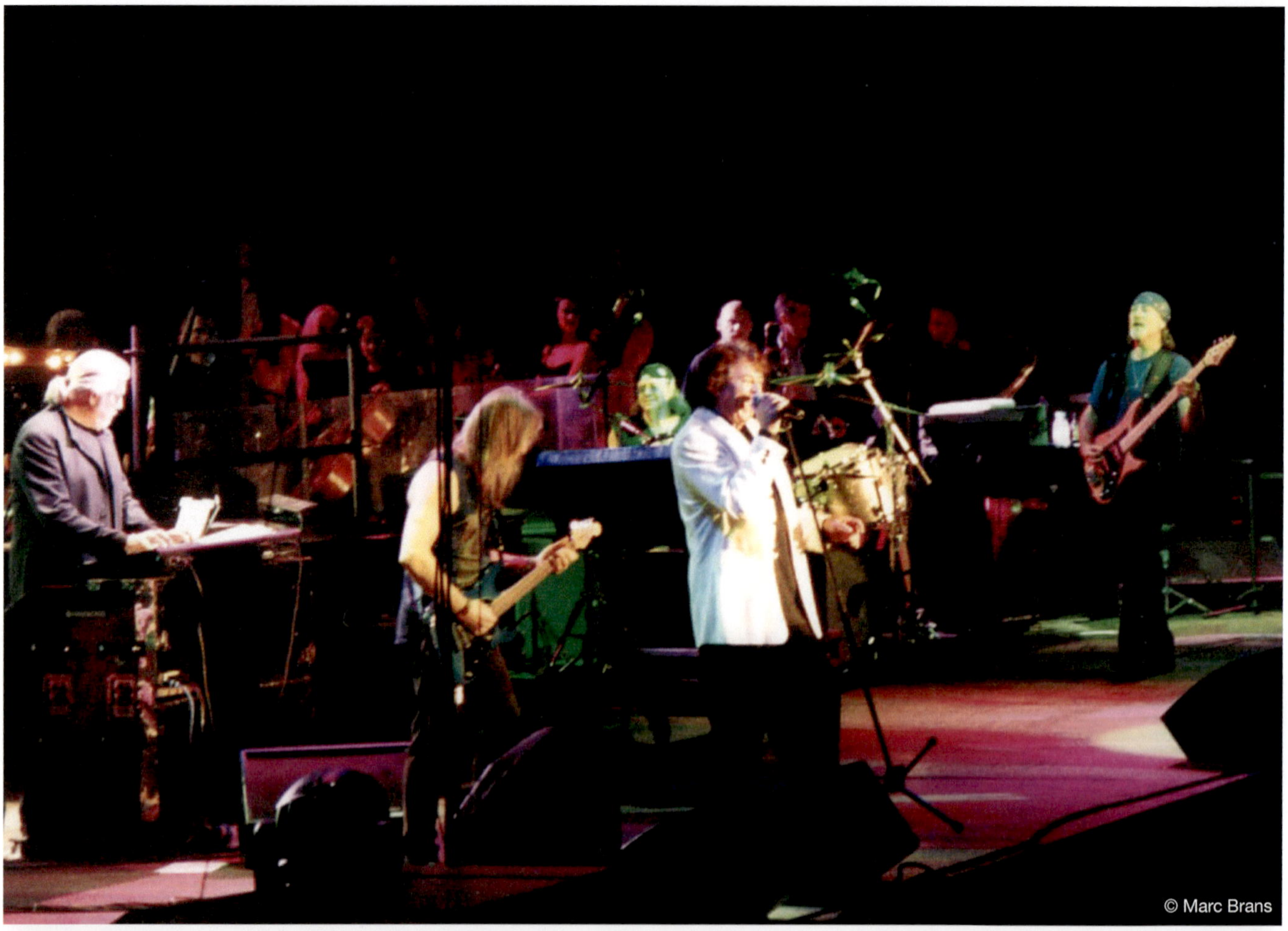
© Marc Brans

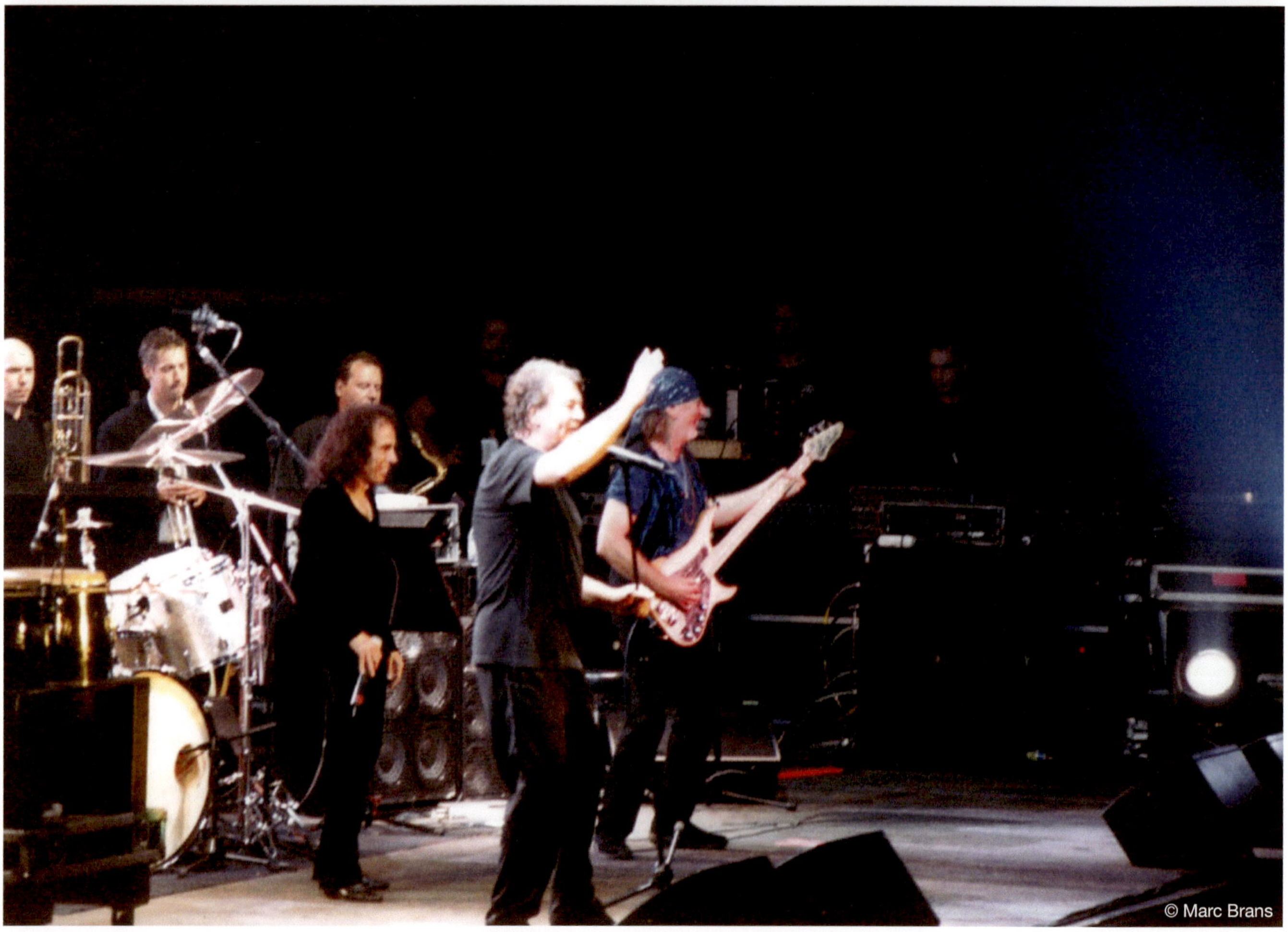
© Marc Brans

Episode Fifteen:
All The Time In The World, 2002-2023

"We played 48 countries last year and it looks like it's gonna be pretty much the same this year."
Interview with Glenn Milligan, 27th March 2009.

If the first eight years of Purple's tenure with Steve Morse brought back stability to the band, the current line-up has now been the longest in the band's entirety by a long margin. Seventeen years and counting, four studio albums and more gigs than most people can recall.

Amongst all that, Ian's appetite for work never diminishes and when Deep Purple does take a break from the road, Ian is out there with other projects, either with a pick up band for the 2008 Gillan's Inn Tour; The 2012 Rock Meets Classic tour as well as a career retrospective film in 2007 and a solo album, One Eye To Morocco in 2009.

Whilst the music business has changed beyond all recognition since Ian first entered it in the sixties, Deep Purple changed tact on their decision to not make anymore studio albums when producer Bob Ezrin enthused about working with them. The 2013 NOW What?! and 2017 Infinite exceeded critics expectations as well as sales forecasts, proving that there is still a marketplace for rock albums in the twenty-first century.

When Deep Purple announced in 2017 that they were embarking on the Long Goodbye Tour, it was specifically intended to be open ended. Whilst ill-health had affected various members of the band in the previous few years, including Ian, a new found well-being and positivity has shown that the long goodbye could still have a lot of mileage left in it.

At an Open Air Festival, Tanzbrunnen, Cologne, 28th August 2002

© Marc Brans

Rosalare, Roeselare Hallen, "Schwung 2003" - Belgium 27th May 2003

Nandrin, "Nandrin Festival" - Belgium 10th August 2003

In Berlin, 20 August 2003 for the promotion of Bananas, the first album with Don Airey that was just about to be released.

At the Spirit of Music open air festival at the Stadion Buchholz in Uster, Switzerland, 2nd July 2004.

SKK Oktyabrsky, Kemerovo, Russian Federation, 8th October 2004

© Aleksandr Timofeev

Mohegan Sun Arena, Uncansville, Connecticut, USA, 23rd June 2005

Performing at Live 8 Canada in Barrie, Ontario on 2nd July, 2005.

At a presentation of Rapture Of The Deep in the Bobby Dazzler pub, Moscow on 13th October 2005

© Mikhail Fomichev (ITAR-TASS News Agency / Alamy Stock Photo)

Teatro Ventaglio Smeraldo, Milan, 15th July 2008

© Massimo Barbaglia (MARKA / Alamy Stock Photo)

"Motor Show Music Festival", ExCel Arena, London, 30th July 2008

© Alan Perry Concert Photography

© Alan Perry Concert Photography

Tatneft Arena, Kasan, Russian Federation, 25th October 2008

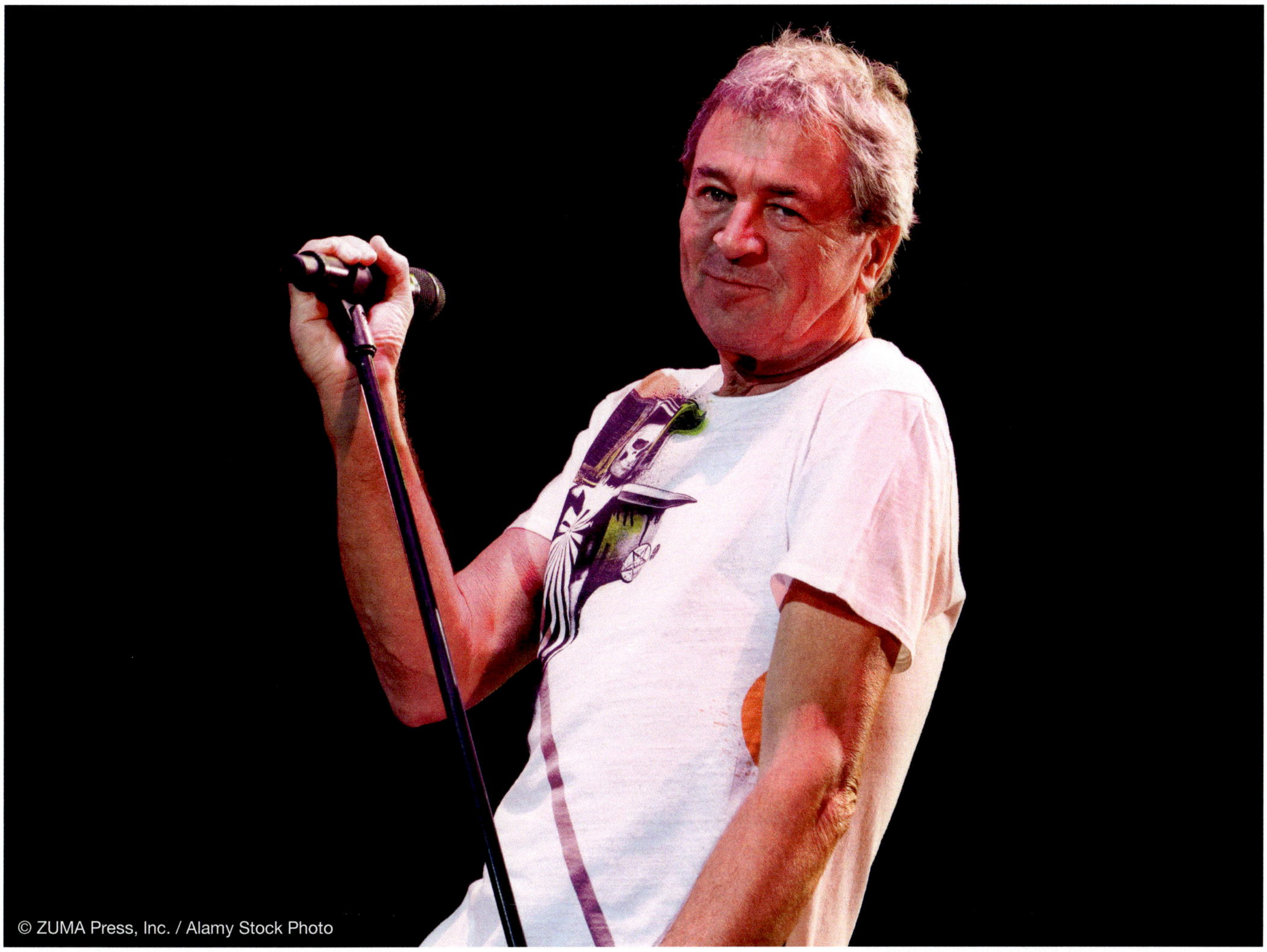

© ZUMA Press, Inc. / Alamy Stock Photo

With conductor Friedemann Riehle of the Symphonic Orchestra of St. Petersburg State Academic Capella after a solo performance at "The Moscow International House of Music", Moscow, Russia on 18th December 2009.

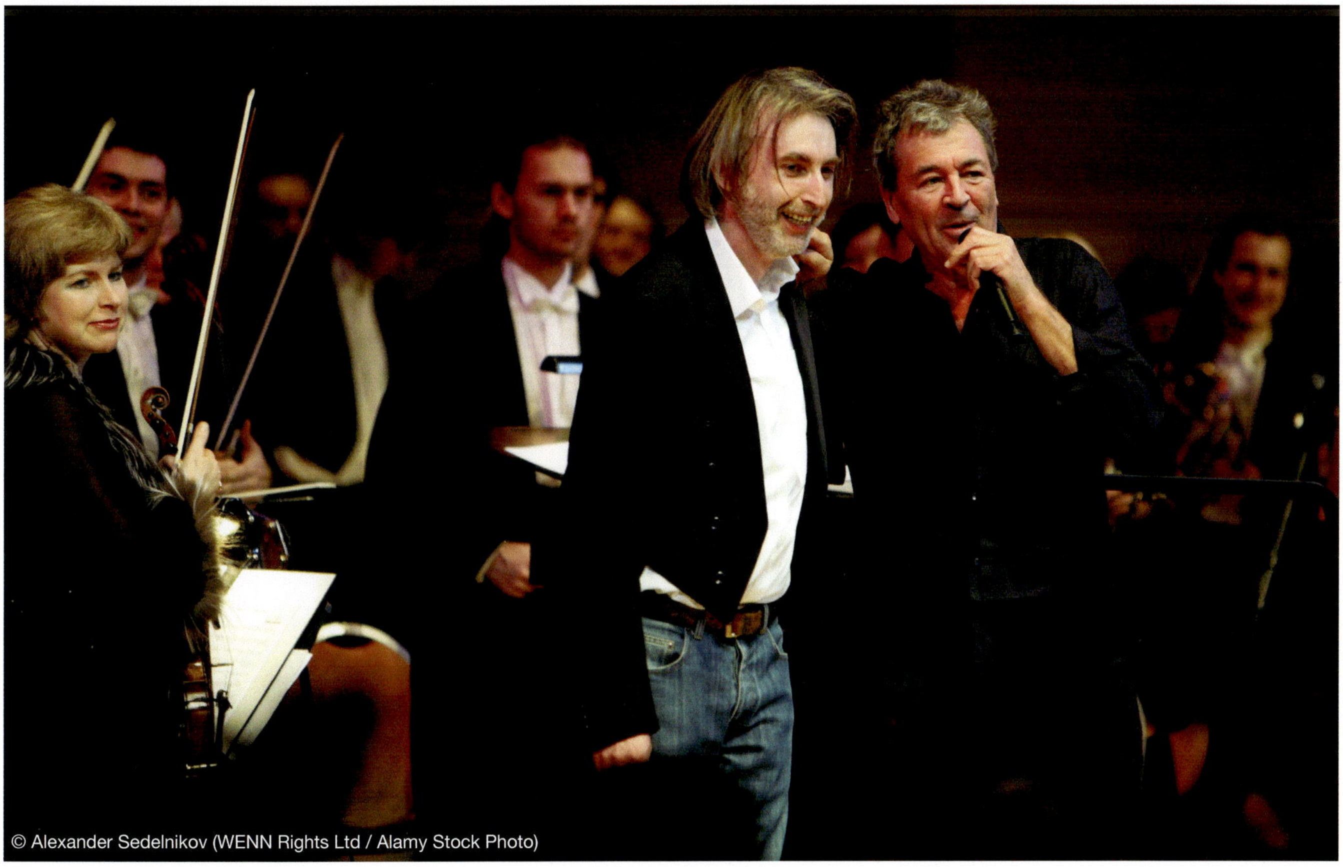

© Alexander Sedelnikov (WENN Rights Ltd / Alamy Stock Photo)

The boys in black at the Nangang Exhibition Hall, World Trade Centre, Taipei, Taiwan 8th May 2010.

© Imaginechina Limited / Alamy Stock Photo

"Now we're going to the palace, dressing up for tea with… The President".
On 23rd March 2011 Deep Purple met Russia's then President Dmitry Medvedev for tea in Gorki, outside Moscow. Medvedev is a huge Deep Purple fan and it was as much of a joy for him, as it was for the band.

© ITAR-TASS/ Vladimir Rodionov

With Robin Beck and Steve Lukather of Toto during the 'Rock meets Classic' concert at the Max-Schmeling-Halle in Berlin, Germany, 17th January 2012.

Photo shoot at East-Side-Gallery in Berlin, Germany, 25th November 2012. This photo session was used for the NOW What?! album.

© Paul Zinken (dpa picture alliance archive / Alamy Stock Photo)

On the set during filming for the video for 'Vincent Price' at the theatre for horror shows at the Berlin Dungeon, 27th April 2013. Also opposite page.

© Britta Pedersen (dpa picture alliance / Alamy Stock Photo)

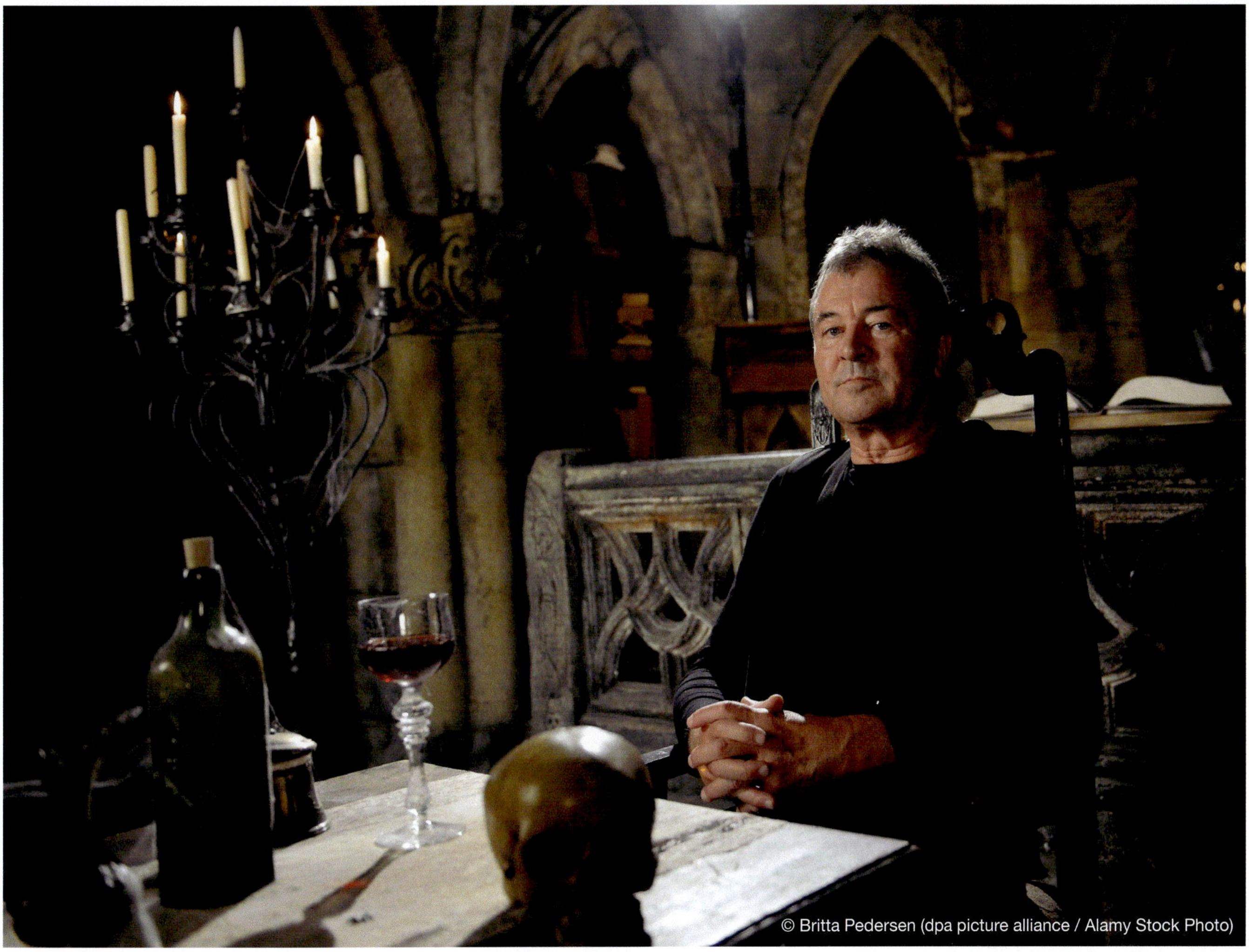

Press conference with Ian Piace for the "18. Mountain Closing Concert" at the Silvretta Arena on the Idalp in Ischgl, Austria, 30th April 2013.

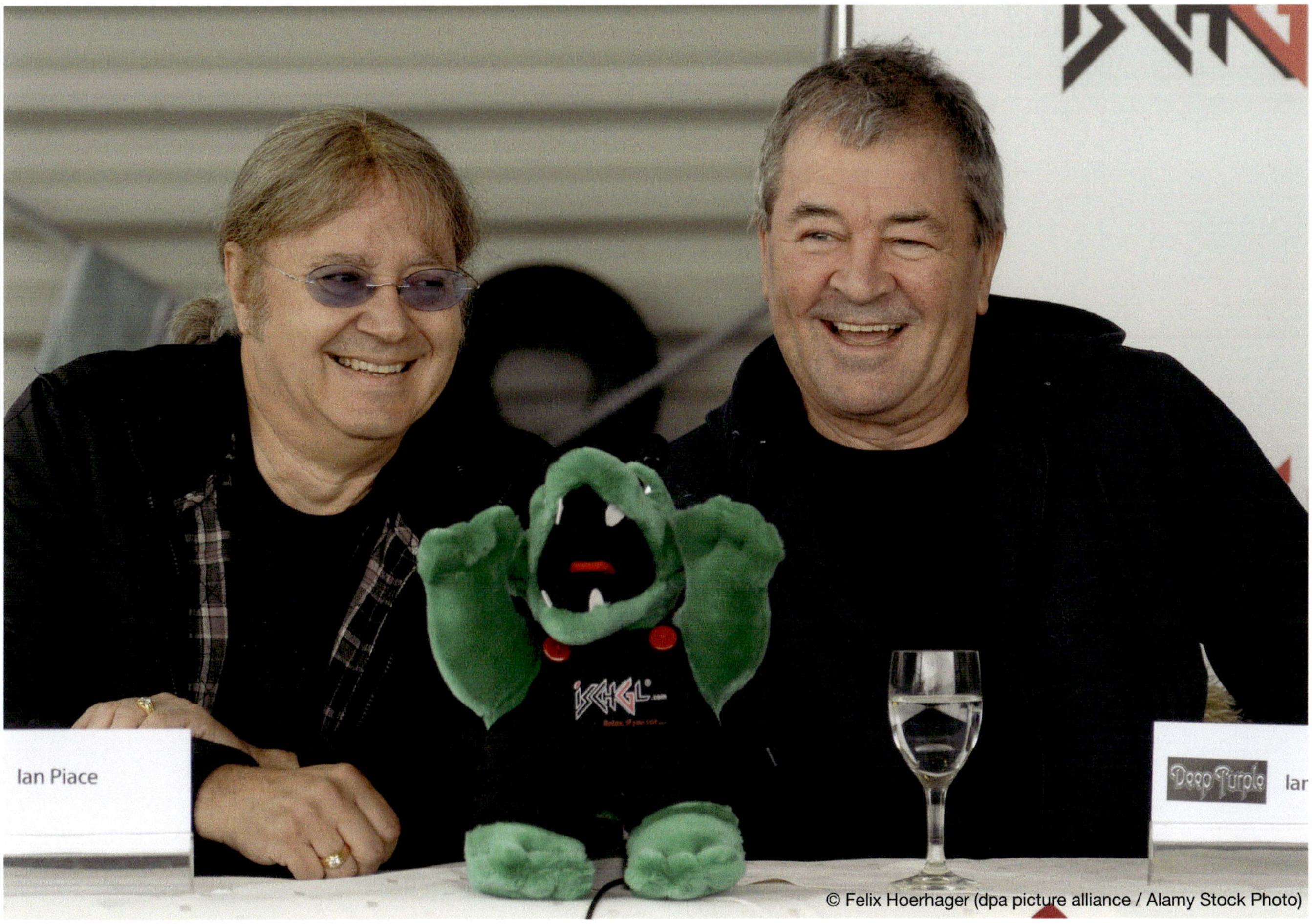

© (Paul Robbins / Alamy Stock Photo)

Lyme Regis, Dorset, England, 6th September, 2014. The 2nd year of the "Guitars on the Beach" event at Lyme Regis brought together guitar players from all over the UK and they set a British record of 3,325 players playing in unison, culminating in 'Smoke on The Water' with Ian.

In the Press Room at the 31st Annual Rock And Roll Hall Of Fame Induction Ceremony 8th April 2016.

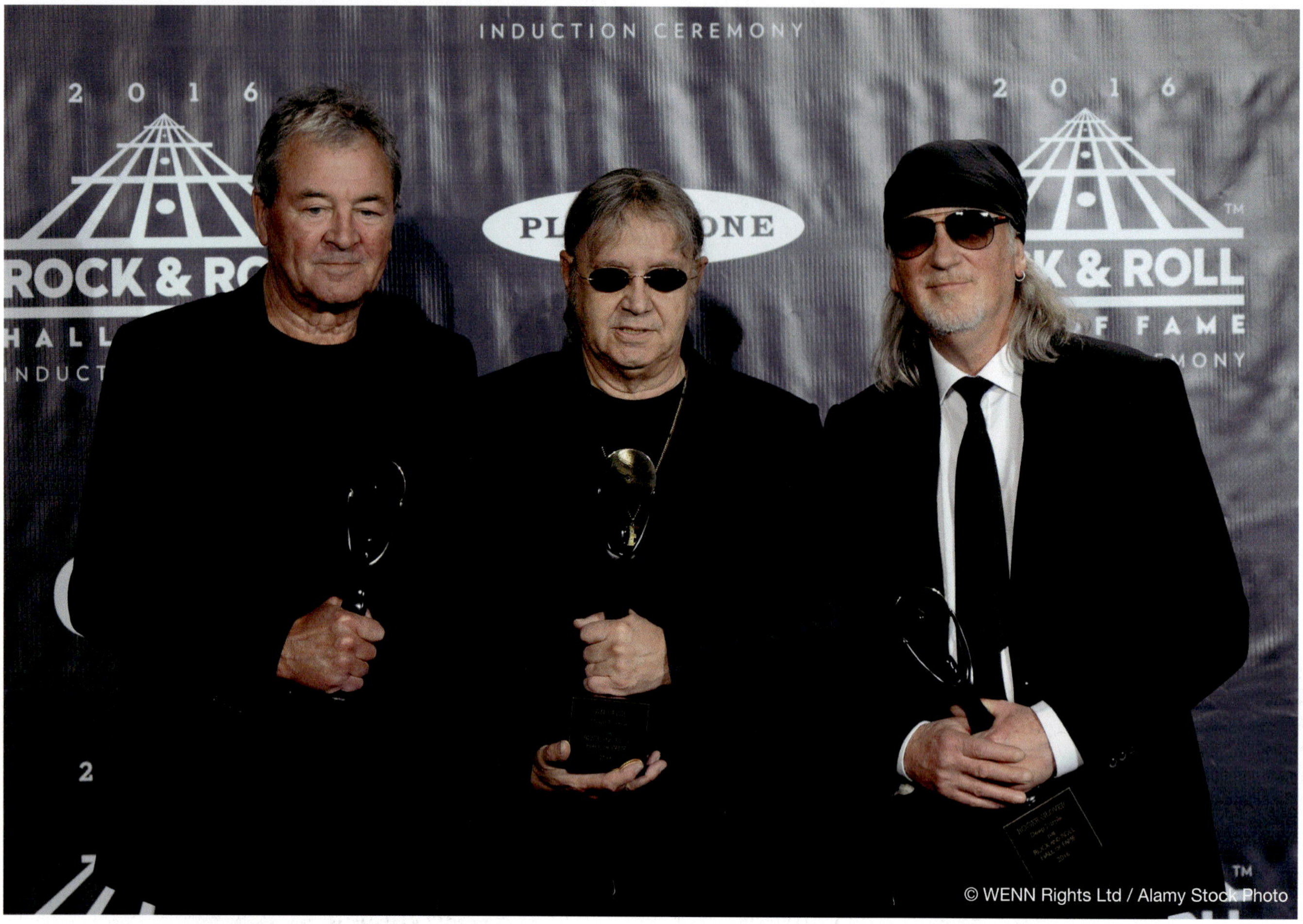

© WENN Rights Ltd / Alamy Stock Photo

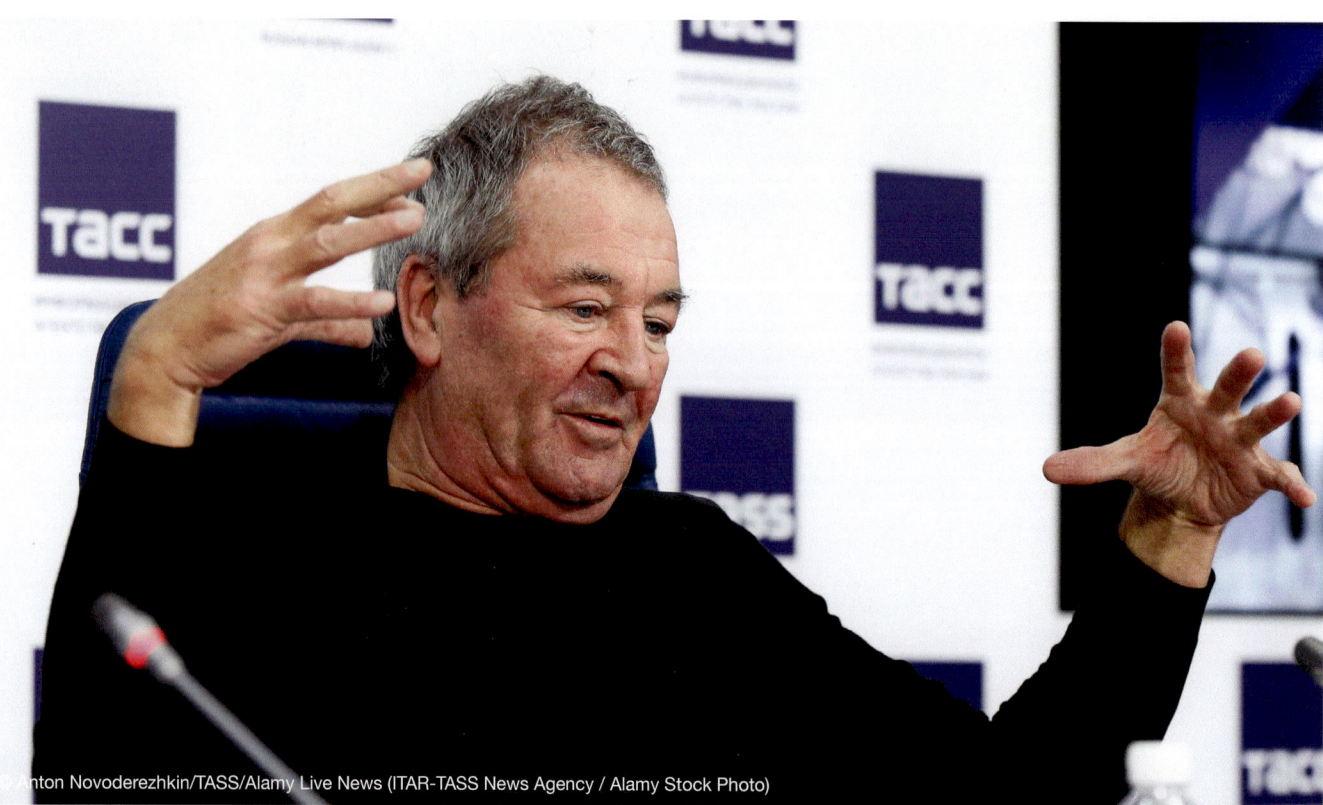

"It was this big".
Whenever there is a break from touring with Deep Purple, Ian always finds something else to do. Here he is in Moscow on 14th November 2016 at the press conference for his show "Ian Gillan sings Deep Purple" that was performed with the Don Airey Band. They played the following night at the State Kremlin Palace.

© Anton Novoderezhkin/TASS/Alamy Live News (ITAR-TASS News Agency / Alamy Stock Photo)

Oktyabrsky Concert Hall, St Petersburg, Russian Federation, 17th November 2016.

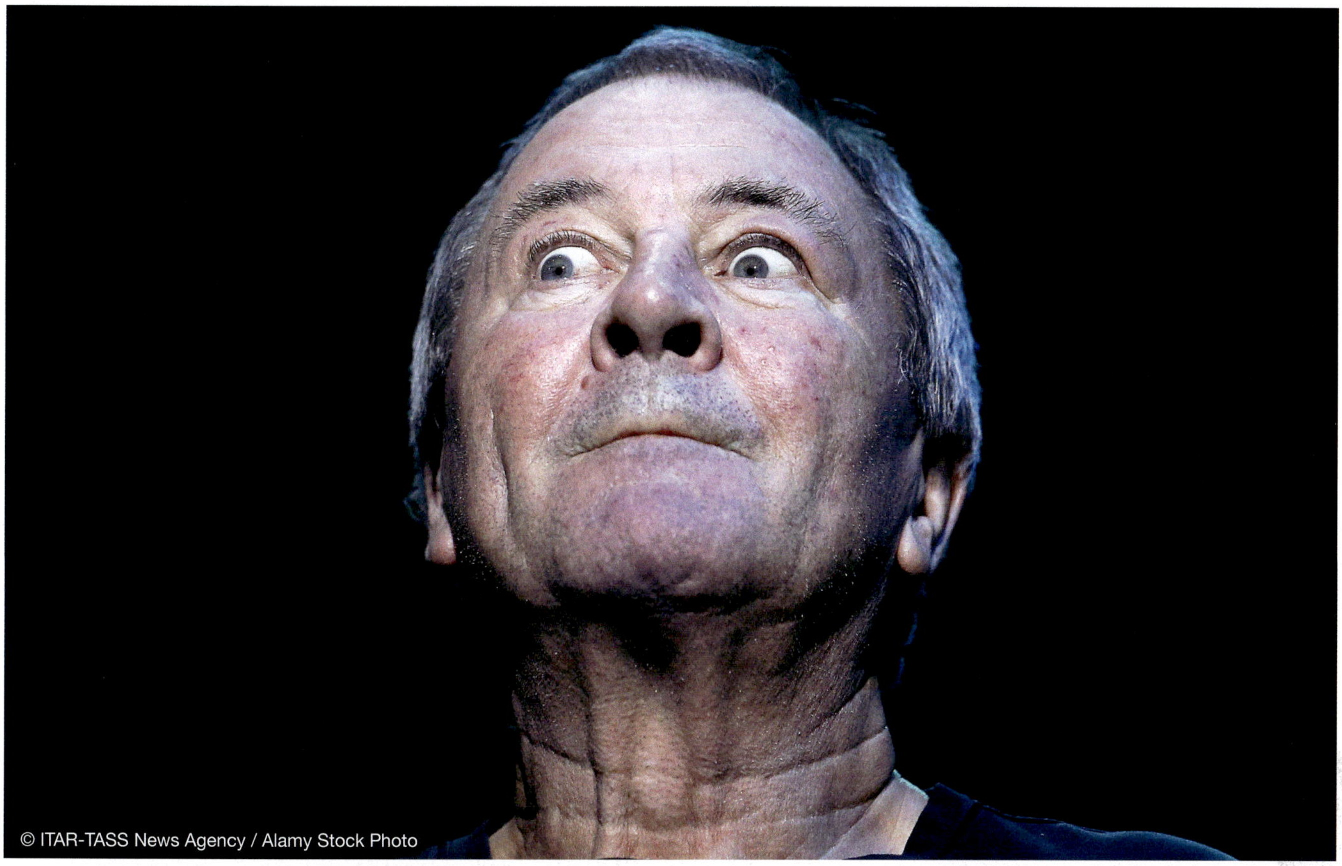

© ITAR-TASS News Agency / Alamy Stock Photo

Arena Zagreb, Croatia, 16th May 2017. The Long Goodbye Tour begins.

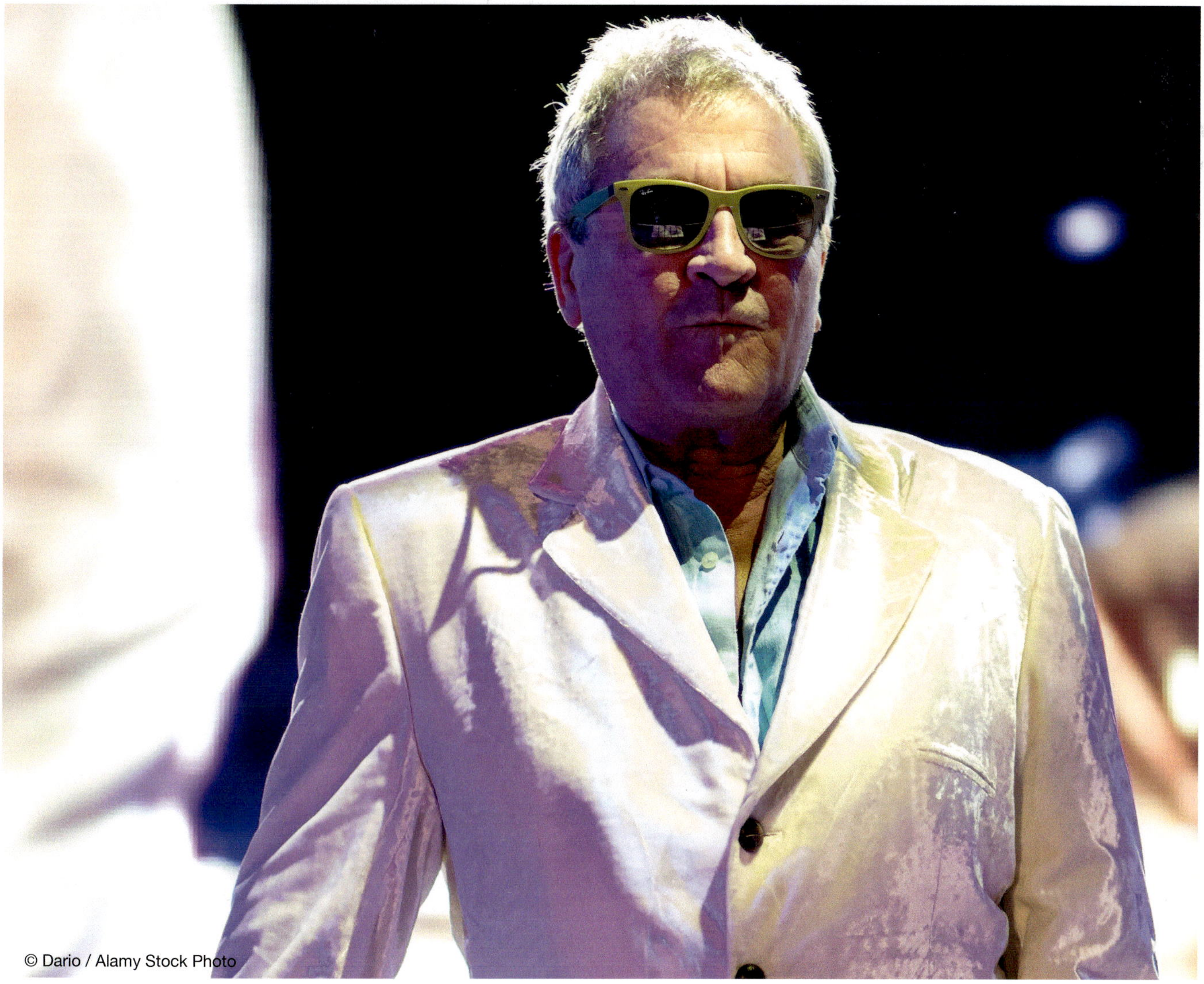

© Dario / Alamy Stock Photo

FivePoint Amphitheatre, Irvine, California, 27th September 2018.

Following a festival show in Mexico on 14th March 2020, Deep Purple had the longest break from touring for decades. All shows were cancelled as the Covid-19 pandemic swept the world. It also delayed the release of Purple's twenty-first studio album *Whoosh!* Recorded before the much of the world went into lockdown, it was eventually released in August 2020.

With the individual band members all grounded, they took to making a new record remote from one another and as a consequence *Turning To Crime* saw Purple having a crack at putting their stamp on a host of songs by other artists.

Live performances eventually resumed in February 2022 but after three shows, the next two were cancelled when three of the band caught the Covid-19 virus. The same month Deep Purple, normally apolitical divorced themselves of the Russian governmental hierarchy that they had been previously associated with.

When they reconvened touring again in May, Steve Morse decided to take a hiatus for family reasons. In came Simon McBride and by September he was officially Deep Purple's new guitarist.

"… Everyone's full of energy. And when the band is cranking as we are, and the audience is giving you help, it's just wonderful stuff. And with Simon, it's just human chemistry. I mean, he's a professional. He's a great player. It didn't take him five minutes to mesh in with us. It was completely natural, and he slotted right in with no problem at all. We didn't even have to think about it."

"… One of the notable things with some of the newer records, we've had difficulty over the years integrating them into the live show. But with the stuff that we've done since we've worked with Bob Ezrin, those albums have been very compatible with the old stuff, so we slipped it in easily. There are two or three in the set right at the moment, and we've got my favourite song that I've ever recorded or written in my entire life in there as well. It's a track from Whoosh!, which is called 'Nothing at All.' We've been putting that in the set, and it is going down a storm. We've also got 'No Need to Shout,' which also has a kind of classic feeling, hard rock riff, and that's working very well too. It's nice, and I feel it's a very well-balanced show at the moment."

Ian Gillan in conversation with Andrew Daley, 27 June 2022

Ian Gillan at 77 with Deep Purple's new guitarist Simon McBride at the Utilita Arena, Birmingham, 25th October 2022.

© Alan Perry Concert Photography